REVIVIFY
Your
HOME

Thank you
So for
inspiring me

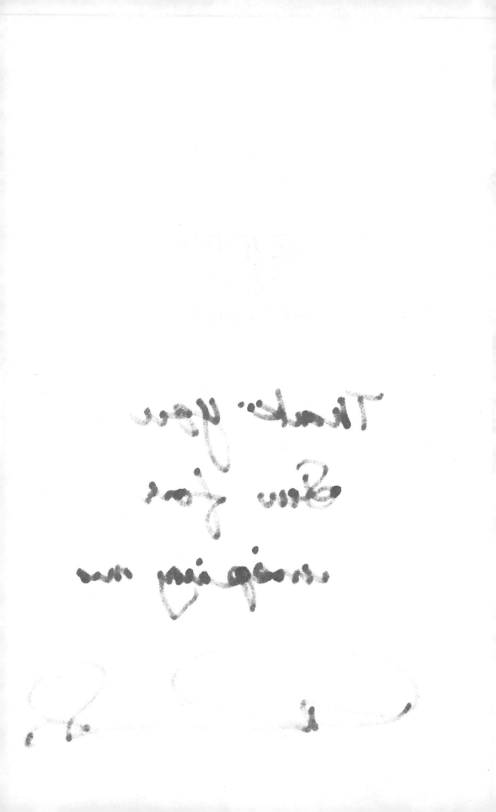

REVIVIFY *Your* HOME

TAKE CONTROL OF YOUR HOME IMPROVEMENT WITH PEACE OF MIND AND LEVEL UP YOUR LIFE

GRACE MASE

ARCHWAY
PUBLISHING

Archway Publishing books may be ordered through booksellers or by contacting:

Archway Publishing
1663 Liberty Drive
Bloomington, IN 47403
www.archwaypublishing.com
1 (888) 242-5904

Photography: Bryan Carpender

BEYREP is a patented technology. Patent No.: US 10,028,206 B2

ISBN: 978-1-4808-7408-4 (sc)
ISBN: 978-1-4808-7406-0 (hc)
ISBN: 978-1-4808-7407-7 (e)

Library of Congress Control Number: 2019933762

Print information available on the last page.

Archway Publishing rev. date: 4/17/2019

Thinking about improving your home? Well, you're in luck! I wrote this book just for YOU - seriously! Whether you want to renovate, remodel, add-on, or build a new home, let me help guide you on your journey. This book will help you understand the process, build your team, and manage your project. *(Note: Out of respect for your time, if you're looking for a DIY how-to textbook or repair manual, this ain't for you.)*

For some people, the uncertainty associated with a home improvement project can be an emotional roller coaster ride. For many of us, riding a roller coaster is a terrifying experience. At the top of the hill, you may feel an incredible rush of excitement washing over you, e.g., signing the contract, seeing the 3D rendering of the final design, and watching the demolition. But when you've dropped down to the bottom, you may feel completely out of control, e.g., moving furniture in a flooded storage room, or washing your dirty dishes in the bathtub while waiting for the plumber to install your sinks and dishwasher. The reality is that home improvement can be an emotional journey, especially if you don't know what to expect and are not prepared for the ride. However, when you are mentally prepared, have a clear roadmap to follow and a prescribed list of things you need to do (and not do), you will feel more in control and will enjoy a smoother ride.

Allow me to show you how you can take control of your home improvement project from start to finish. Through this journey together, I'll help you to prepare mentally and emotionally, and plan strategically. I'll equip you with the knowledge you need, help you get your arms around your project, hire a compatible and qualified team, manage it with confidence and peace of mind, and get the outcome you envision.

Whether this is your first home improvement project, or you've been through many projects, there are always things you wish you'd known or had more control over. I'll walk you through the process, and be there with you every step of the way.

Ready, Set ... Go!

Contents

PART IV: OH, ONE MORE THING

REVIVIFY

(/rēˈvivəˌfī/ verb. To give new life to something.)

Introduction

Hey, you! Yes, I'm talking to **YOU**, the person holding this book. Congrats on taking the first step towards improving your home! Your home is an extraordinary place; it's where you inspire and support people who matter to you, nourish and recharge, create memories with family and friends, and build a better life. Presumably, you picked up this book because you want to improve your home with confidence and enjoy peace of mind as you go through the process. That's awesome — we're on the same page!

First off, since this is the introduction, allow me to introduce myself: I'm Grace — it's so nice to meet you! I'm excited and honored to share this journey with you. I've been where you are. I went through a home renovation nightmare … but I turned it around and lived to tell the tale. (Don't worry, I'll tell you all about it in later chapters.) Now, you get to benefit from my experience and learn from my mistakes, so you don't make them yourself.

Throughout my renovation experience, one thought was constant: No one should have to suffer through a home improvement nightmare - *there ought to be a better way.*

Then I remembered my first successful and profound home improvement experience ... (Yes, I am going to bring you back with me to my early childhood.) I was a young girl, I recall walking with my dad through the construction site of our new home. My parents poured their entire life savings into our new home. It's a mid-rise building in a newly developed area suburb. In an early Sunday morning, I followed my dad, and we stepped into an empty family room with rebar puncturing through the concrete floors, I looked up to my dad and saw how proud and happy it made him as he witnessed his dream of a better future transforming into a reality. My dad didn't openly express emotions very often, so this was an incredibly powerful moment for both of us — and one that had a huge impact on me; it propelled me to pursue a career in architecture so that I could help bring that pure joy and sense of accomplishment to other people.

Between graduating from UC Berkeley and Yale University with degrees in architecture, I worked as a Principal Architect for UC Berkeley. In this role, I managed multiple projects entirely from design to construction. These experiences taught me a great deal about how to mentally prepare my clients (brilliant department heads, their entire faculty, staff, and the student body), and how to plan the project, streamline the design and construction process, and collaborate with diverse teams to get building projects done on time — and on budget. Since the projects were state-funded, there wasn't a lot of room for error. It was a great training ground to overcome any obstacle with creative solutions and manage projects effectively and efficiently.

While at grad school, the Dean wanted to build a website for the school. I took the job because I was paying my way through school (Hey, a girl's gotta hustle!). While learning to build the website, I was fascinated by how people interacted with technology, and technology can help to solve a real-life problem efficiently when it's implemented correctly. After grad school, I transitioned into the technology sector, where my design and architecture skills were redirected to designing and building large, complicated software applications such as Yahoo! Search Marketing solution, Beachbody eCommerce platforms, and apps. I've spent the past two decades sharpening my design and product development skills, and now, I get to use them in exciting new ways. Plus, my years of hard work taught me the value of a dollar, as well as how to spend it wisely.

Fast forward a few years, and I found myself on my own home renovation rollercoaster. I was almost taken for a ride. I doubted myself, felt embarrassed and ashamed because I thought I knew better.

I shared my experiences with a close friend, who is extremely intelligent and always on top of things. She seemed uncomfortable, and I noticed her body tensed up, and she put a pillow in front of her as she slumped down. There was a long pause, then she started to speak, her voice cracked, and she was visibly angry. She recalled a poor experience with her contractor who told her "Don't you worry your pretty little head about it. You don't know what you're talking about."

It was extremely demoralizing for her. Like me, she also thought she should be able to manage a project without a lot of drama. The floodgate of pain, self-doubt, frustrations, and resentment poured out of her. To make it worse, this occurred just as she started her chemotherapy treatment. She didn't have the energy to fight him. At the same time, she was too embarrassed and too proud to admit that her project went off the rails under her watch.

After the setback, she tried to bury the pain and decided to suffer in silence. Unfortunately, her wound was never healed properly. After we exchanged our stories, we both felt relieved knowing that we weren't alone, and our experiences weren't isolated. We started our healing process together.

I have asked many homeowners to share their stories, and although they all had different experiences, but the end results were the same. They all reminded me of a bad breakup with a range of emotions, such as self-doubts, hurt, embarrassed, disappointed, resentment, and feeling out of control.

These conversations helped me to realize that home improvement projects can have an emotional impact on one's life. Though I survived it, I knew I had to learn from these painful lessons, and turn them into something positive, so I developed a personalized online system to help busy homeowners like me manage their home improvement projects more easily.

Did you know that Homeowners spend more than $300 billion a year on residential renovations? And that their dissatisfaction with home improvement construction has ranked as one of the top three consumer complaints for the past twenty years, according to the Consumer Federation of America? Clearly, my frustrating home reno project was not an isolated event.

These facts helped me realize that I had an obligation to share my proven method with you so that you can use these tools to take control of your project with confidence and peace of mind. This is the reason WHY I decided to write this book.

Now that you know the *Reader's Digest* version of my life story and my WHY, let's talk about why it's so important for you to know *your* WHY, HOW, and WHAT …

Think of your home renovation as a journey; it's like going on a road trip. Would you just pile into your car and hit the road without a destination or a navigation app? Hopefully not.

The most important part of planning your road trip is determining your destination. Then, you need directions to know where you're going so that you don't take the wrong exit and end up on a detour — or at the wrong destination.

Then there are other preparations you need to make for your journey. You have to make sure the car is fueled up, the tires are properly inflated, the fluids topped off, and everything is checked out for a smooth trip. You do all this so you don't break down on the highway because that would delay you reaching your destination, inconvenience you, and result in the trip going over budget. (Also, don't forget to bring snacks and drinks. And of course, you need to have an awesome playlist.)

Now, who is taking this journey with you? Make sure you have the right people in the right seats — and that everyone on-board is going to the same place before you leave. You don't want to be driving to Six Flags, and then only to discover on the road that two of the passengers thought you were going to Disneyland. That's some major miscommunication.

Now, back to your renovation project. Think about your answers to these questions:

> **WHY** - Why do you want to improve your home?

> **HOW** - How will your improvement project impact your life and people around you?

> **WHAT** - What's your home improvement goal and priorities? What's your project budget?

> **WHO** - Who will be part of this journey with you to help you achieve your goal(s)? Are they on board with you?

Answering these questions is essential for this journey. Don't worry, you don't need to have all the answers right now, so don't even think about putting this book down! We're going to work through this together — and you may find that some of the answers may reveal themselves more clearly as we go along.

Let's build the momentum and move forward toward your end

goal ... whatever that may be. Take a moment to savor this; it's an exciting time for you — you're about to **REVIVIFY** your home and level up your life! Don't worry, I've got your back. I've been through this, and I'll be with you every step along the way to help you through it, too!

Are you ready? If you've read this far, you must be ready. (You look super ready to me. Ready and confident. Like someone who is READY. I really like that top, by the way.)

Well, take a deep breath and let's go!

(That was me — standing on the concrete foundation in my Sunday best.)
Photography: An-Ching Tsao

PART I

Ready

1   Connect Your WHY/FI

I know what you're probably thinking: "What the heck is **WHY/FI**?!?"

No, that's not a typo; it's an easy and fun concept that you'll be using throughout this process (and maybe even in other areas of your life). Even better, you control the signal strength of this **WHY/FI**, you can connect to it anywhere, and best of all, it won't affect your data plan!

It's a simple process that will help you discover your true **WHY**. It clarifies your thinking by motivating you to drill down and continue to examine your **WHY** until you arrive at the root issue or problem that needs to be resolved. Through this process, you will also discover the **HOWs** to achieve your **WHY**.

A very wise man named Simon Sinek said: **"Start with WHY."** His mantra is going to help kick off your journey; because identifying your WHY is essential to your success, I'm going to reinforce it with a quote from another great twentieth-century philosopher …

"WHY?" – Annie Lennox, 1992

I first stumbled across this concept of asking **WHY** as a Graduate Fellow Teaching Assistant for Professor Vincent Scully's History of Art course. He encouraged all of his Teaching Assistants to ask questions to spark our students' curious minds, which would lead to a deeper understanding and appreciation. Jumping on that bandwagon, I sounded like a two-year-old toddler repeatedly asking "WHY?" to my students as we examined each art piece or artifact. After a while, I noticed that after the fifth consecutive WHY? their body posture changed, their head would tilt slightly, their eyes would light up, and a smile would emerge. Their excitement was contagious and helped to elevate my own appreciation of the art piece. We all experienced our own A-HA! moment.

I experimented with different numbers of WHY?, but consistently found that five consecutive questions would result in that interesting phenomena. While I observed the behavior, I still didn't quite understand and appreciate the full power of WHY?

A few years later I came across a TED talk "Start with WHY" by Simon Sinek.

He explained why it's essential to start with **WHY**, and it inspired me to participate in the "Finding Your WHY" workshop with Jen Waldman, Peter Docker, and Christina Alessi to articulate my **WHY** — and that workshop profoundly changed my life.

WHY = Purpose, mission, or reason of being

Many people start a project focusing on what they want to do and without ever asking the simple but essential question that is imperative to their success — "WHY?" Then they find themselves lost in a sea of decisions and choices, and feel overwhelmed or lost, it is often because they didn't have sight of **WHY** they're doing what they're doing.

So, to set you up for success in your home improvement project, the first step you need to take is to answer this simple question to get to the root of the matter:

WHY do you want to renovate your home?

Don't worry, I'm not going to judge you; I just want to understand your WHY so I can meet you where you're at and support you at the right level.

To determine the **WHY**, there are also some **HOWs** and **WHATs** you'll need to ask that will help you to clarify your WHY. Here, I'll show you what I mean …

Example:

>**WHY** are you embarking on this renovation journey?

>**HOW** do you want to feel once the renovation project is finished?

>**WHAT** do you want to accomplish within your budget for your home renovation project?

To make it easier, I'll even go first and share with you my **WHY**:

>*To empower you to own your potential and stand in your greatness, so that you can celebrate your present joyfully and upgrade your future.*

That's **WHY** I've written this book. The other reason is that I've personally been through a home renovation nightmare. I've been there. I went through a miserable experience, learned some tough lessons, and came out on the other side wiser — and now, I want to share my experiences so you can learn from my mistakes and avoid the same pitfalls.

Adding some HOWs can also help you to clarify your **WHY**.

My **HOWs**:

- Help you map out your journey strategically and emotionally so you can get **READY** to navigate the process.
- Provide you the knowledge and **SET** you up with the right tools to harness your creativity and amplify your power.
- Put you on the optimal path to **GO** forward and make your dream into a reality.

Those are my **WHY** and **HOWs**. Yes, that's pretty much what this book is about. (Well, that — plus the fact that the title will help you sound legit leading edge and super intelligent when you use it at the next meetup with your nearest and dearest. You'll feel like a boss-ass home renovator. You're welcome.)

Anytime you ask a WHY question, you need to follow it up with more **WHY** questions until you arrive at a specific (and often simplified) **WHY**. This process helps you quickly go from general to granular — and you can usually get there by asking five **WHY** questions. (See? **WHY/FI!**)

Here's an example I've borrowed from Jon, a colleague who became one of my clients. He and his family live in a single-family home near the Tournament of Roses Parade route in Pasadena, California.

He came to me, frustrated, saying only, "We need to build an addition onto our home." When I inquired WHY he responded with a general overview of his problem: "Our home isn't big enough."

I pressed him by following up with several WHY questions, guiding him to refine his thinking and really get to the root of the frustration. Here's the breakdown — it was so dramatic, I'm going to treat it like a scene from a movie:

FADE IN:

INT. GRACE'S STARTUP OFFICE - DAY

GRACE sits at her desk, typing on her laptop, working on the manuscript of the very book that you're currently reading. JON enters her office, flustered and frustrated and sits down in a chair.

GRACE
Hey, Jon. Is something wrong? You seem ... (pausing) stressed. What's going on?

JON
I can't take it anymore. We need to build an addition onto our home.

GRACE (curiously)
Okay. Tell me more.

JON
Our home isn't big enough. My kids don't have enough room. Right now, they're on top of each other. Literally.

GRACE
WHY are they on top of each other?

JON
They're currently sharing a room.

GRACE
WHY are they sharing a room? I thought
you have a 3 bedroom house?

JON
Well... they're actually sharing OUR room.

GRACE
WHY are they sharing YOUR room? Are they
sleeping in your master bedroom?

JON (exasperated)
Yes. The kids sleep in the same room
with my wife and me.

GRACE (confused)
Okay, help me to understand WHY they
aren't sleeping in their own room.

JON (sheepishly)
Well, their rooms are really small, and
their toys and clothes are taking up
the entire room. So they camp out in
our room. And now we have no privacy. I
miss spending quiet time with my wife.

GRACE (calmly)
So, WHY do you need an addition to your
home? What's the REAL reason WHY?

JON (nodding, understanding)
Well I want to expand my kids' rooms,
add a lot of built-in storage space and

a play area for them   then my kids can move out of our effing bedroom. Oh, I also want to remodel our master bedroom. (Pause) I guess the real reason WHY is just SO that my wife and I can enjoy a quiet space to recharge, in order to be better parents for our kids and better partners for each other! (Big smile)

GRACE
Congratulations, Jon. You've just con-nected Your WHY/FI!

Aaaaannnnndddd SCENE!

Your **WHY/FI** statement should be meaningful and personal. It should start with what you plan to do, and then describe the pos-itive impact. You have to dig deep to pull out your true WHY. In the previous scenario, the **WHY/FI** for Jon's project is for him and his wife to recharge, so that they can be better parents for their kids and better partners for each other. His **HOW** (to activate his WHY) is to expand kids' rooms, add a lot storage space, and playroom, and remodel their master bedroom to create a quiet space to recharge for him and his wife.

Here's a streamlined example of how to connect your WHY/FI:

Statement: I want to renovate my kitchen and make it bigger.

WHY 1? Because the kitchen is too small, and I want more counter space.

WHY 2? Because I feel cramped, and there's not enough space to prepare a meal. I'd like to have a more open plan kitchen.

WHY 3? Because I want to fit more people in the kitchen comfortably.

WHY 4? Because I enjoy preparing meals and spending time with family and friends, especially while cooking for them.

WHY/FI = Create an open plan kitchen to prepare meals with at least 10 of my family and friends, so that I can enjoy spending quality time with them, creating new memories, improving the quality of our lives together.

BOOM! See how quick and easy that was? With a quick drill-down and some follow up WHY questions, you went from general to specific, uncovering the real WHY, which lends both perspective and an emotional attachment to the desired end result. The HOW is to *renovate and create more counter space and simple circulation flow to accommodate more people in my kitchen.*

You'll be surprised how easy it'll be to get into the groove of connecting your WHY/FI and how quickly it will become a good habit. By connecting your WHY/FI, you'll be driving clarity, and you'll start making well-informed decisions, which will increase your confidence and will ultimately make you that much happier with the end result.

"Regardless of WHAT we do in our lives, our WHY— our driving purpose, cause or belief—never changes."
— Simon Sinek, Author

Insider Tips

Your **WHY/FI** is exactly that: it's uniquely yours. To get the hang of it, you may want to work with a friend, spouse, partner, children, or family member who can help you to ask questions objectively, and then ask them to repeat back to you what they heard (like a mirror ... that talks, or reflects back) for you to discover your **WHY**.

Below are three **HOW** questions to get you going. Visualize and think about the end result of your improved home. From there, hold those feelings, then figure out your **WHY 1**, then dig deeper to come up with your **WHY/FI**:

Close your eyes and picture being in your newly improved home ... What do you see? What other things can you sense? Record those feelings. *(Hint: If you are by yourself, use your smartphone to record a voice memo to capture your own words.)*

- How do you want to feel in your newly improved home? (e.g., peaceful, safe, energetic, organized, spacious, open, inspiring, warm, comfortable, etc.)
- How do you want your newly improved home to feel? (e.g., like a creative hub, or like a warm, cozy ski cabin, etc.)
- How do you want people who matter to you to feel in your newly improved home? (e.g., inviting, inclusive, fun, friendly, calm, open, etc.)

There are no right or wrong answers. This is for your eyes only, so there's no pressure.

Why do you want to revivify your home?

WHY 1

WHY 2

WHY 3

WHY 4

WHY/FI

2 Whose Elephant is This?!?
Acknowledge Your Fears

Let's talk about the elephant in the room: you're afraid. And that's okay, because everyone has fears, especially when undertaking something involving your home.

Great ideas to improve your home are everywhere you look. Whether it's glossy magazine covers in the grocery store checkout line, or blogs and websites, or even the latest DIY images on Houzz, Pinterest and Instagram, there's no shortage of inspiration. Turn on the TV and you'll find multiple networks dedicated to home improvements, design ideas, and aspirational programming. (Heck, there are entire apps allowing you virtually redesign a room, or an entire house, or even design it from scratch; but that's not going to help you achieve your goal. It's time to do it for real!)

It seems like everyone else is making over their homes and their lives, yet you are stagnant. Great ideas are a dime a dozen, but only great execution will turn a great idea into great reality. You may have similar goals and aspirations — why aren't you taking action? What's holding you back? You want to get out on the floor and dance, but you're being a wallflower, staring longingly at the happy couples busting their moves. Why are you watching, scrolling, liking, and wishing, when you could be making your goals a reality? My guess is there's a common culprit: **FEAR**.

It's important to know that you're not alone. Millions of people dream, design, imagine, and even envy home improvement projects without ever pulling the trigger because they're afraid. Of the unknown, of the cost, of the interruption to their life, of getting taken advantage of, of getting caught in a never-ending renovation project. Their paralysis prevents them from seeing the joy that awaits them on the other side of their remodel.

You may not realize that fear is holding you back, because you have a laundry list of seemingly valid reasons why you aren't forging ahead to make your goals a reality, but the unpleasant truth is that you're scared. (Also, denial isn't a river in Africa — that's The Nile.) Being scared is okay, though. Because home improvements can be scary! Just ask anyone who's lived through them. Ask anyone in the industry who's been responsible for completing them.

Your home is your sanctuary, your safe haven, and your biggest asset — both financially and emotionally. In order to make the improvements, now you're going to invite a bunch of strangers to break and tear it apart as part of the process to build something better. Oh, don't forget the fun fact that you actually get to pay for the privilege of having your personal space invaded and dismantled in a less than tidy manner! It's no wonder that strikes fear in your heart and mind! Just remember, you're not alone.

Naming That Elephant, Identifying Your Fear

Okay, let's talk. The thought of undertaking a home improvement might seem overwhelming, but it likely comes down to one specific thing that powers that pesky little fear demon in your brain, and is effectively stopping you from moving forward. Here are the top five common themes:

- My budget is really tight.
- I don't know what I don't know.

- I don't want to get screwed over by a contractor.
- I'm really busy.
- I'm unsure about how to get started.

You need to name the elephant in the room, and you can start by answering this question:

What Powers Your Fear Demon?

For some people, it's money. Are you afraid the project will exceed your budget? Are you afraid the unqualified, glorified gardener or handyman will take you for a ride, robbing you blind in the process, and leaving you high and dry with the project unfinished? Are you uncertain about how to find and hire the qualified and compatible professionals to help you achieve your vision? If you care about the design, should you hire an architect or a designer?

For others, they're afraid of letting strangers into their home to do the work. Are you able to trust the contractors? Will they consider your ideas and incorporate them? Or, will they simply relegate you to the sidelines while they assert their own agenda over your space?

For others, that pesky fear demon might be focused on time. How long is it *really* going to take? How are you supposed to live without a kitchen for six weeks? What if the project goes over schedule? How will you and your family survive the project without ending up at each other's throats?

Stop. Take a long, deep, calming breath. Now take another one. And one more. There … doesn't that feel better? These are all valid questions, but before you get yourself all worked up over them, you need to realize that these questions will have answers, and you can rest assured we'll work through them together.

Let me help you shut down your inner fear demon and tell it

to take a hike. Remember, I'm here for you. I'll help you navigate through the process and find reputable and qualified building/design professionals (let's be unbelievably cool and call them Pros) for the job, so you don't need to play Russian roulette with an online directory list. I'm also going to help you get an accurate roadmap of what will happen to your home throughout the project — and help you hold your Pros accountable. No surprises, no pitfalls. Just effective communication.

So, if you want to learn how to move forward confidently, first you need to determine exactly what it is that's holding you back, then confront it. Returning to that question, ask yourself: "What powers my fear demon?" Once you answer yourself honestly, you can face your fear and move past it into action.

Get Real With Yourself/Self-Reflection

Now that you've identified what powers your fear demon, acknowledging your fears and confronting them isn't going to be easy. Or pleasant. It's not something you've been looking forward to doing, but that's exactly what's holding you back. Much like getting a shot in the arm, the anticipation is usually much worse than the actual shot. You're scared of the pain, but getting that shot is never as bad as you've built it up to be in your mind. Now, take a deep breath and consider your answer to that question.

Next, ask yourself why you're allowing the answer to keep you from pulling the trigger on your home upgrades. Are you truly going to allow your goals and dreams to be held hostage by fears and concerns that are so easily assuaged? (Spoiler alert: No, you're not ... because you have me on your team, and I've got your back.)

Once you identify the fears that prevent you from moving forward, you can begin to address them. Better yet, as you start to make a plan to confront and move past those fears, they start to lose any power they held over you. Let's go back to the earlier examples:

- My budget is really tight - Like anything you have done in other parts of your life, you managed your money, e.g., buying a car, planning a vacation, etc. You choose to spend on things that matter to you. Improving your home isn't about "having more" or "spending more"; it's about optimizing to make things better so you can gain more with what you have. In your home improvement, you'll set a budget. It's an investment you're making for your future, and the improvements you'll make will have tremendous impact on your life. When you plan ahead, you'll likely save money. Think of it like this: you're adding value to your home and your life!

- I don't know what I don't know - You may not know much NOW, but that's about to change! Like everything you've accomplished, you start with limited knowledge. Along the way, you ask questions and learn as you go. You know you're really resourceful. In no time, you'll figure out the answers to all of your questions.

- I don't want to get screwed over - Of course! No one wants to get screwed over. You've gone through life this far and know how to surround yourself with experts who know more and can guide you through the process without getting screwed. Do some homework like checking with your State License Board to see if the folks who are interested in your project are licensed. The more you check if they're legit, the less chance you will get screwed over.

- I'm really busy - The reality is that home improvement can be time-consuming. However, you'll make time for things that will provide pleasure or meaningfully impact your life. With a bit of planning, you won't have to waste time fixing mistakes. In fact, you'll likely get time back. You've been thinking about your home improvement project for a while, and know your home improvement will have an incredible result. If you don't invest a bit of time now for a better future, will you regret it later?

- I'm unsure about how to get started - Well, you're in the right place. I'm here to shine a light on the path to get you started. You've already done the hardest part — you made a decision with intention and clear purpose to improve your home and upgrade your life. You're reading this book, the rest is totally manageable, and we'll get through this together.

That's pretty reasonable right? You've got this.

Every issue has a solution, and now that you've identified your issue (or issues — there's no shame in having more than one issue to deal with), you can get on track to take action toward creating the home you've always dreamed of having. Your **WHY** will provide the clarity you need to guide you through many of the decisions along the way. It's like a lantern, cutting through the darkness and illuminating the path to your hopes, dreams, and aspirations. (I wanted to give you an inspiring visual, so there you go. You have chills right now, don't you? Mission accomplished.)

Get To The Root Of The Issue

We've already discussed the most common reason why people hesitate to jump into a renovation — fear, but what caused that fear in the first place? You may have had a bad experience in the past, and hope it will be better the next time around. Or, you've never been through a home improvement project before, but maybe you've heard enough horror stories from other people. What about it is so terrifying that you're afraid to get into this one? For some, it's merely the fear of the unknown. However, for others, there may be deeper issues at play — issues that have nothing to do with home improvements.

Your Conscious and Subconscious Minds

You likely think of yourself as a rational, reasonable person — at least most of the time. The idea of home improvement looks excellent on paper. It makes perfect sense to tweak, upgrade, and improve different aspects of your home. You'll increase the value of your home, you'll get a more comfortable living space, and these improvements may even favorably impact your health and well-being. That sounds like a big freakin' WIN/WIN, right? So, then what's the haps — why are you hesitating?

Well, the answer lies in your subconscious mind: the thoughts, feelings, and emotions that lie below your conscious thoughts. Often, without you realizing it, your subconscious mind could be sabotaging your efforts by attempting to protect you from pain. In this case, I'm talking about the pain of inconvenience, stress, and unrest, which are all part of any home improvement process. Because it's not something that you're entirely aware of, it's also something that can be difficult to understand.

For example, let's say you've never dealt with home improvements before, and you have a great deal of anxiety about being ripped off by a contractor. You've never hired an architect, designer or contractor before, but your friends, family, or neighbors who have successfully completed renovation projects of their own are happy to help. Perhaps they've even given you referrals to the people who made their projects happen, yet you're still nervous. Why? On the surface, you have no reason to be afraid. You have no personal negative experience to draw from; you only have positive anecdotes from friends and family or raving online reviews, as well as positive references. So what's holding you back?

Well, your subconscious mind is a devious thing, and this is where it comes into play. In typical rational thought, your logical mind wouldn't correlate a past negative event in an unrelated field with your new project. However, your subconscious mind might. It's almost like your subconscious mind has a mind of its own. There may be other factors influencing your subconsciousness. The reality is that not everyone's expectation in quality and preferences are the same; different people have different communication styles and methods. As a result, your friend's referral may be perfectly great for her or him, but it may not be perfect for you.

For example, let's say that 10 years ago, you wanted to buy a new car and the salesman jerked you around, raised the prices, or just generally ripped you off. The experience was painful and humiliating, and not something you ever want to go through again. Now, your conscious mind may come up with some strategies to prevent this from happening again, such as bringing a friend along with you or getting recommendations from people you trust to avoid ending up in the same situation.

However, your subconscious mind wants to protect you from the situations that you aren't aware of. (That's why it's subconscious — DUH!) In this case, you're hiring a contractor to work on your home. As important as buying a new car is, your home is even more critical; the stakes are much higher. Your subconscious mind is attempting to protect you from being hurt again, and plants seeds of doubt and misgiving. As a result, you fear to hire the wrong person for the job, even with all the positive references and surrounding circumstances. Because your conscious mind is not in control, your subconscious mind takes over and attempts to do the job, minimizing risk on your behalf. Therefore, your uniqueness requires a personalized match so you can find the right Pro to handle your job.

Taking Charge

Now you see why I'm urging you to identify and confront your fears. To get to the root of the issue and take control back from your subconscious mind, you need to decisively name what you're afraid of so you can put together a plan to move past it. If you're scared of being taken advantage of, then rather than choose a course of inaction, you can seek out tools that will help you manage the process and feel secure and in control every step of the way.

Of course, this is much easier said than done. It's time to make YOU a priority. You owe it to yourself to upgrade your home and, in turn, your life. To get started, you have to look within and determine what's holding you back. Only then will you be able to put a plan in action that will take you from hesitant to passionately engaged, as you work toward your newly improved space and life.

"It is impossible to live without failing at something, unless you live so cautiously that you might as well not have lived at all, in which case you have failed by default."
- J. K. Rowling, Author

Insider Tips

Fear is universal: we've all experienced being held captive by our own terrors. To reach your destination, first, you need to know where you are and acknowledge your current fears. The best way to work through your fears is to start with pen and paper so that you can see them — and then conquer them.

Admitting you're afraid of something isn't a weakness. It's empowering to face your fears. In fact, acknowledging them and then conquering those fears is one of the bravest things you can do.

This FEAR CRUSHING WORKSHEET will help you put your fears on paper. Get them out of your system. This simple act of writing them down makes them less scary. It enables you to understand where you're at, what you need to face, and what actions you need to take. There is plenty of space for this exercise. Get ready to move past it and kick fear's a$$ so you can get your life the upgrade you deserve!

FEAR CRUSHING WORKSHEET

Your Top Fears	Rank 1 - 10 (1 = highest, 10 = lowest)	Actions to Overcome
I'm afraid of ... of getting taken advantage of ...	1	Review the contract in detail, ask questions when you're not sure, and run it by an attorney. Document everything.

3 Know Thyself!
How Your Personality Type Influences Your Decisions

It's much easier and more fun to collaborate with someone who is compatible with you, in addition to being qualified to do the job you need. Then, no matter how big the issues may be, you will always find ways to resolve them together. On the other hand, when you work with someone who is not compatible, small issues can be blown out of proportion. Hence, hiring the right pro, one who is compatible with you and qualified to perform your home improvement project, is critical. *(I used "hence" because this chapter is a little academic but in a fun way.)*

Consider this fact: while marriages last on average only about eight years *(separate after seven years and one year to process the divorce)*, the average U.S. homeowner keeps their home for about fifteen years. Think about how much time and effort you put into finding and selecting your partner. You want to be matched with someone who understands your vision, respects and shares your values, and wants to help you to level up. You'll want to look for many of those same qualities as you seek a partnership with the Pros to improve the home that you'll live in for many years.

Personality is one of the key attributes that can be a good indicator of compatibility. Knowing yourself is an essential first step in understanding how to work well with others. There are all kinds of personality assessments out there, but there are a few you may be familiar with: DISC model, Myers-Briggs, and the Big Five *(not the sporting goods retailer)*. All of the personality assessment is a framework to group people with similar traits and identify some of the common behavior types. They are relatively straightforward; to help uncover your personality traits, you answer a series of questions that help gauge how you will react in certain situations.

Most people take the test for fun, often posting their personality types for others to see on their LinkedIn, social media, and online dating profiles. For Myers-Briggs, one may look at the results and say, "Oh, they totally get me! I'm an INTJ! I'm an introvert -- that's why I like to recharge after parties!" But did you know that your personality type might be influencing how you react in situations? It could also be affecting how you approach decision-making, respond to different life situations, and impact the outcome of your home improvements.

When you embark on the home improvement project, you will likely collaborate with others who may have different personality traits. To help others to understand what you want, you need to know how to communicate with them effectively; more specifically how the others prefer to receive the information. As a person who likes to get things done quickly, I was working with a Pro, who needed time to process information. I didn't realize it at that time, and I expected him to respond quickly. A couple of days went by, and he didn't answer. To me, he doesn't seem to appreciate the same urgency as I do. So I naturally assumed that he was willfully delaying the project. Fortunately, we learned about each other's personality traits and were able to work through it. In many situations, personality differences may create unnecessary tension and undesirable friction, which could snowball and lead to something more intense.

To understand the basics of different personality traits is like acquire a different language. When you get more familiar with the personality traits, you will be more effective in communicating with others, because you will understand how others would want to receive your message. Your communication goal is to convey what you want so the others can be on the same page to work with you. Everyone is different, and everyone is not you. There are no best personality traits (even though for those who are a "D" type in DISC model, you may think you have the best personality traits). To understand different personality traits will help you to be mindful where others are coming from, be mindful how you usually react and think through how you may need to recalibrate your response to a situation so that all of you are on the same page. We need different traits to work together to achieve project success.

DISC Model

DISC model is a behavior personality assessment tool based on the work of psychologist <u>William Marston</u>'s "<u>The Emotions of Normal People</u>" in 1928, which centers on four different personality traits which are: Dominance (D), Inspiring (I), Supportive (S), and Cautious (C). The DISC model is one of the simplest to understand. The foundation of the DISC Model is based on two observations about how people usually behave:

> Observation #1:
> **Outgoing vs. Reserved**
> This trait is like a person's "internal pace" ranging from extrovert to introvert. Some people may seem ready to "go" and "dive in" quickly, while others tend to engage at their slowly or more cautiously pace.

> Observation # 2:
> **Task-Oriented vs. People-Oriented**
> This trait is like a person's "external priority" guiding people to focus on either tasks or other people.

Some people focus on getting things done (tasks); others are more tuned-in to the people around them and their feelings.

Again, there are no right or wrong or good or bad. The two observations are merely different behavior styles. Everyone has different styles; that is entirely okay and normal. Like the 2x2 diagram with four quadrants illustrated below, some may be more extreme than others. So keep in mind, there is a varying degree of intensity with these two observations. In general, everyone has some of all four of these tendencies in different situations, at different times when interacting with different people. Most of us have 1 or 2 of these tendencies that seem to fit well in our everyday behavior. The balance of these four tendencies shapes the way each person "sees" a situation and respond to it accordingly with their traits.

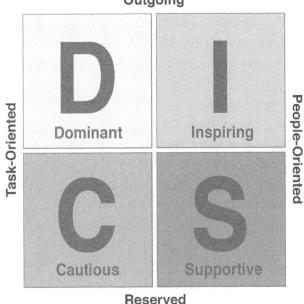

Fig. 1 DISC Model.

Dominant "D"

An outgoing, task-oriented individual will be focused on getting to the bottom line as quickly as possible, and accomplishing tasks. For anyone who is "D" type, her/his motto is GET IT DONE! If this is you, be mindful and considerate with other people's emotions and feelings. When you work with a "D" type of person, RESPECT her/his time and focus on RESULTS.

Inspiring "I"

An outgoing, people-oriented individual loves to socialize, interact, and have fun. This person focuses on what others may think of her/him. For anyone who is "I" type, her/his motto is LOOK AT ME! If this is you, make a conscious effort to follow through and complete the task at hand. When you work with an "I" type of person, who enjoy being the center of attention, ADMIRE her/his contribution and RECOGNIZE the effort.

Supportive "S"

A reserved, people-oriented individual will enjoy helping or supporting other people and working together as a team. This type of person is the hardest to spot in a group setting but the easiest to get along. For anyone who is "S" type, her/his motto is ACT OF KINDNESS. If this is you, learn to get a bit more comfortable with the unknowns or changes and don't take things personally. When you work with an "S" type of person, be FRIENDLY and show your APPRECIATION of her/his support.

Cautious "C"

A reserved, task-oriented individual will seek consistency, value and quality information. This person focuses on being correct and accurate. For anyone who is "C" type, her/his motto is TRUTH PREVAILS. If this is you, learn to relax a bit and cut others some slack. When working with a "C" type of person, who takes pride in

TRUSTWORTHY and INTEGRITY, acknowledge the quality and accuracy will go a long way.

Just for fun, next time you're at the airport waiting for your flight, take a look around, and see if you can spot the following types:

- "D" type person (outgoing and task-oriented) wearing a simple solid outfit, striding towards the gate right before they close while talking on a mobile.
- "I" type person (outgoing and people-oriented) dressed in a bright and colorful outfit or flashy accessory that calls for attention, talking loudly to others or on a mobile phone.
- "S" type person (reserved and people-oriented) wearing soft or neutral color casual outfit, who may be smiling and approachable.
- "C" type person (reserved and task-oriented) wearing conservative and traditional outfit trying to blend in, working on a laptop.

Myers-Briggs

The MBTI was constructed by Katharine Cook Briggs and her daughter Isabel Briggs Myers. It is based on the conceptual theory proposed by Carl Jung, based on the four primary psychological functions — sensation, intuition, feeling, and thinking. The combination of the four traits creates 16 different personality types. Each of these types helps describe who you are. Now, here's a caveat: these tests are not designed to be the gospel truth or the end-all, be-all, definitive explanation of who you are as a person. Your life experiences also play a part of how you react to certain situations, but knowing a little bit about your personality can help you understand (or even anticipate) how you may react to certain situations, and as a result, help you turn those situations to your advantage.

Introvert vs. Extravert

The first letters in the group are either I or E, meaning you are either an Introvert, a person that needs alone time to recharge, or an Extrovert, a person who recharges by being around others.

For Introverts, the idea of hiring someone to work on their homes may be an intimidating aspect of any project. If you find yourself nervous about a person coming into your home, remind yourself of this:

- You do NOT need to spend every minute with this person
- This person will be a member of the team working on your home — not someone you need to please or take orders from

If you find yourself working with a person with introvert traits:

- Be considerate of their space and time
- Be efficient and focus on the project

Extroverts, on the other hand, may find the idea of having someone in their homes exciting. Just keep in mind that this person is there to do a job, not for a social occasion. If you find yourself working with a person with extrovert traits, remember this:

- You're paying them and their time equals your money, so spend it wisely!
- By all means, establish a rapport and build a relationship to make the process more comfortable, but don't create a forced friendship.

Intuitive vs. Sensing

The next letter in your group is either going to be an N for Intuitive or S for Sensing. If you are Intuitive, you'll likely focus on the bigger picture. If you are a Sensor, you'll probably focus on details. N's may find home improvements more enjoyable than S types, just because they can step back and trust that the results will be worth it. S types, however, may get caught up in small details. If you find yourself focusing too much on minutiae in getting this project off the ground, remind yourself that it's the result that matters most, and try to get a sense of what it will take to get there. If you find yourself working with a person with Intuitive traits, you can talk through the idea, and she/he will get excited about the big thinking. For a person with Sensing traits, you need to show her/him any visual aid to help illustrate your point.

Feelers vs. Thinkers

The third letter in the group is for Feelers and Thinkers. Feelers make decisions based more on how they feel about them, while Thinkers can be more objective. In this grouping, it's often the Feelers that may encounter more obstacles in moving toward their home improvement goal because they feel so intensely about their home and their place in it. Thinkers can step back more efficiently, making the process easier in this regard.

If you find yourself getting emotional about the project, try to determine what is causing such strong emotional reactions. What is it about the project that's upsetting you? It's okay to have feelings of stress, anxiety, or uncertainty -- just don't let them consume you or derail the project. Acknowledge those feelings, then deal with them using reason and communication. Keep your eyes on the prize: your newly renovated home!

If you find yourself working with a person with Feeler trait, you will need to acknowledge the emotional reactions and work through any potential issues together. Working with Thinkers, you can talk through any potential problems methodically.

Perceivers vs. Judgers

Rounding out each personality tag is either the letter P for the Perceivers or J for the Judgers. Both groups may find themselves encountering issues with home improvements here, but for very different reasons.

Perceivers may find themselves getting worked up about things that haven't happened yet. Will the shipment be delayed? What will the contractor find when she/he opens the wall? Will I be ripped off? It's easy for a Perceiver to get mired downplaying the "what if?" game, which can lead to difficulty getting the project going. You may need to try stepping back slightly from the project, relying on a partner or team member to help you through. If you find yourself working with a person with Perceive trait, talk through the possible issues and decide how to manage those situations together.

Judgers, however, tend to scrutinize things as they are taking place, or just after they are done. For Judgers, it's not the idea of the home improvement that's the obstacle; it's getting it done to their satisfaction. If this is you, try to focus on the bigger picture and let go of some of the smaller details to help things fall more neatly into place. If you find yourself working with a person with Judge trait, you can help her/him to understand your expectations, so together you can move forward with the project.

Big Five

The Big Five personality traits were identified by Ernest Tupes and Christal in the late 1950s. They defined five factors, represented by the acronym OCEAN: Openness to experience, Conscientiousness, Extraversion, Agreeableness, and Neuroticism. These sound funny, but can actually provide valuable insights.

Openness to experience

People who are Open to Experience tend to be more creative, curious, and crave a variety of experiences, rather than routine.

Those with low openness tend to be data-driven, prefer what they know, and can be perceived to be close-minded. Those open to new experiences may find the home improvement process exciting, as it taps into their creativity and novelty. Those with low openness may find a home improvement process daunting, as it requires them to go outside their comfort zone.

Conscientiousness

People with high conscientiousness are planners who tend to be organized and dependable. These types may experience stress in planning out all the details. Take care to be open to suggestions from others, and not to appear stubborn and inflexible. Those on the other end of the spectrum need to make an effort to pay attention to the plan, even if the details don't interest them, to ensure a positive outcome.

Extraversion

People who are Energetic, Assertive, Sociability and the tendency to seek stimulation in the company of others, and talkativeness. High extraversion is often perceived as attention-seeking and domineering. Low extraversion causes a reserved, reflective personality, which can be seen as aloof or self-absorbed. Extroverted people may appear more dominant in social settings, as opposed to introverted people in this setting.

Agreeableness

People who are high in Agreeableness tend to cooperate and get along well with others. While these types are trusting, they may need to push themselves to get the outcome they desire. Those with low agreeableness can be argumentative and perceived as challenging and distrustful of others. Both will need to be mindful of their tendencies as they collaborate with their team throughout the project.

Neuroticism

People who are highly in neurotic measures the degree to which you experience stress and anxiety under challenging situations. Their emotional reaction can overwhelm your good judgment if you let it. Those with high stability appear calm through the storm but may need to work to demonstrate that they are interested and engaged.

Know Thyself

We have just scratched the surface of the dynamics involved in personality traits. As mentioned before, everyone is different. Personality traits are complex, made up of different facets. So, do yourself a favor and really take the time to get to know your personality, be mindful of other people's personality traits, and understand how to connect with them the way they prefer to engage with you. Read the full assessment of your personality type and try to recognize where it rings most true for you in the way you react to different situations. Having this understanding of how you operate might help you navigate the different personalities working on the project, as well as help anticipate and identify potential problems before they have a chance to develop. Who needs a crystal ball when you can just truly know thyself?!?

"Art is all a matter of personality."
- Marcel Duchamp, Artist

"My personality is humongous."
- Cardi B, Musician

Insider Tips

These worksheets will help you understand why you do things the way you do, learn what really drives and inspires you, build more meaningful collaboration with others, and better navigate through the situations you encounter. We all have experience working with people who are compatible, and no matter how big the problem may be, somehow things just work out. On the other hand, when we work with people who are not compatible, small issues seem to get blown out of proportion and result in unnecessary drama. Considering home improvement is such a huge emotional and financial investment if you have an opportunity to collaborate with design and/or building professionals who are compatible with you to have a high probability in achieving project success, why wouldn't you?!

We're not trying to psychoanalyze you, we're not trying to get our Ph.D. – we're just trying to give you context and help you better understand and be more self-aware of your tendencies so you can more effectively interact with people who get what you need.

MY PERSONALITY *(select one per pair)*

Myers-Briggs

Pair 1		
Introvert you typically prefer to need alone time to recharge	OR	**Extrovert** you recharge by being around others
Pair 2		
Intuitive you tend to focus on the bigger picture	OR	**Sensing** you tend to focus on details

Pair 3

Feelers   OR   **Thinkers**

you tend to make decisions based more on how you feel

you tend to make decisions based on objective facts

Pair 4

Perceivers   OR   **Judgers**

you may get worked up about things that haven't happened yet

you may tend to scrutinize things as they are taking place

Big Five

	Traits	
Close-Minded Practical Conventional Prefers Routine	**Openness** ← →	_Open-Minded_ Curious Imaginative Open to New Ideas
Unconscientious Disorganized Impulsive Carefree	**Conscientiousness** ← →	_Conscientious_ Organized Responsible Dependable
Introverted Quiet Withdrawn Reserved	**Extraversion** ← →	_Extraverted_ Outgoing Energetic Seeks Adventure
Disagreeable Critical Uncooperative Suspicious	**Agreeableness** ← →	_Agreeable_ Considerate Trusting Empathic
Emotional Stable Calm Stable Confident	**Neuroticism** ← →	_Neurotic_ Anxious Moody Lower Self-Confidence

4 Broken Window Syndrome

Now that you've identified your home improvement **WHY** grab your passport and embark on the journey of home improvement — it's time to map out your journey plan. Many people have fears, yet eventually push them aside to tackle the issue, usually after a specific event. For example, a major leak occurs, and while investigating it, you discover that you have a mold issue. It motivated you to bundle the leak issue as part of a complete remodel.

In addition to your fears, what else might be keeping you from looking around, genuinely seeing the state of your home, and deciding it's time for some improvements? There's a likely culprit: Broken Window Syndrome.

It's not easy, but by taking the time to really look at your home and see what will improve it. You'll find that the end results will be that much more satisfying once you do.

You'd think that with the wealth of information around surrounding home improvements, that most people would come away with a better understanding of what's involved. Unfortunately, this isn't always the case.

Things like HGTV and magazines are so staged and scripted that they end up giving homeowners a completely unrealistic look at what a home improvement really looks like. In the show, you see the designer casually doodling on a pad while the contractor rips things out and the new materials arrive in minutes. Maybe there's a quick scene where one of the Pros needs to make a phone call to the homeowner alerting them of a significant, unexpected expense, which the Pro is always apologetic for and the homeowner always accepts graciously.

In reality, though, home improvements can take a lot of unexpected twists and turns. They can also take much longer and cost a lot more money than you may be expecting. For this reason, one of the most effective ways of contributing to your project's success — and keeping your own sanity through the process — is to manage your expectations.

Explaining the Problem

If a window were to break suddenly in your home, you'd do your best to get it fixed right away, wouldn't you? Most people would. But what if you can't fix it right away? Maybe you don't have the money right now. "It's not that big of a deal," you tell yourself. "Next month, I'll have the cash, and then I can fix the windows." (See also other chart-toppers like "The check's in the mail," "I'm in complete control and can stop any time," and "I swear, it wasn't my fault — somebody else did it.")

Then, every day of the ensuing month, you look at those broken windows, and it's both frustrating and upsetting. So much so that eventually, you stop seeing them. You walk past them every day, and you look at them, but you don't really register the fact that they're in need of repair. This is your brain's way of trying to protect itself from undue stress. It knows the windows are broken, but since you can't do anything about it right this second, it tricks you into ignoring them.

That's a nifty trick, but unfortunately, the longer you go without "seeing" the broken windows, the more they become normalized to you. They begin to blend in and seem like part of the house, the way it's always been, so any sense of urgency to repair them dissipates. And the only thing broke is the promises you made to yourself to upgrade your home and your life.

The good news is that, in most cases, broken windows actually do get repaired. However, that outdated kitchen, that leaky bathroom, that cumbersome floor plan can all be ignored in the same way. Remember, it was your fear that stopped you from tackling these issues when you first noticed them. Now, your brain is trying to keep you from stressing about them, tricking you into not seeing them in the same way you did before. They cease to become a priority and go into limbo as you become easily distracted by everything else in your life.

Dealing with the Issue

Whether we realize it or not, we've all dealt with a bout of broken window syndrome at some point. When living with a home that isn't quite what you want it to be, whether it's disorganized, poorly laid out, or falling down around your ears, denial becomes an attractive option for even the most tuned-in person. Coupled with the fears that hold many people back from beginning the renovation in the first place, broken window syndrome can have you stuck in a holding pattern for years. Often, you remain in this stagnation until another more severe and more costly event — such as a burst pipe or structural damage — pushes you to take action.

Thankfully, dealing with a broken window syndrome is simple; it requires objectivity and a curious mind. You know how you want to live and how space can work for you or what doesn't work. You can invite a trusted friend or family member over, and ask them to look at the rooms of your home with you. Or comb through every square foot yourself like a detective, try to see your home through the eyes of someone that doesn't live there and doesn't see it every day. This step is what most architects and designers will do when you meet them; they ask questions and look around your home. The fresh perspective and honesty might surprise you, as the little things you previously overlooked have now become glaringly obvious.

Congratulations! By taking this important step, you are confronting and moving past your fears and into a mindset that will allow you to start taking charge of your home improvement process. (Hold for applause!)

You're checking your fluids and packing up the car as you prepare to embark on this journey. Forge ahead and let's get on the road!

"Take a chance! All life is a chance. The person who goes the furthest is generally the one who is willing to do and dare."
- Dale Carnegie, Author

"What you do today can improve all your tomorrows."
- Ralph Marston, Author

Insider Tips

The best way to achieve project success is to understand your home improvement motivation and set a clear, prioritized plan. By doing so, you'll get inspired, set targets, drive decisions, and get results. I created this Home Improvement Wish List worksheet to help you brainstorm and prioritize. You can go around your place, make a wish list of areas that need improvement, and then for each issue, rank the importance and the factors (Design, Cost, or Time) that matter the most to you. Please start with your **WHY/FI** that you developed in the previous worksheet, and let's tackle your Home Improvement Wish List!

HOME IMPROVEMENT WISH LIST

Your Home Improvement WHY	Areas of Improvement & Its Current Condition	Factor Matters Most: Design, Cost, Time
Example: I want to spend more quality time entertaining and cooking with people I love, creating memories in my kitchen.	Outdated small kitchen -> open plan kitchen with more surface space	Design

5 Check the Rearview Mirror Before You Move Forward

You've identified your broken windows, now let's check out those new windows to replace them. To get a better view of the new, it's often helpful to stroll down memory lane. You know how hearing a particular song or seeing a scene from a particular movie can trigger specific emotions and memories, transporting you back to that moment in time? That's what I'm talking about. Think about the childhood homes you lived in growing up. Many of those places made impressions on you. As you recall other places, such as your grandma's house, best friends' pool house, vacation home, hotels, or fun places you have visited in the past, you'll realize how they made lasting imprints on your memory. Think about what made them so memorable:

- Why did you like about those places?
- How did those places make your life fun or enjoyable?
- What were the specifics that made it memorable and enjoyable for you?
- Do you want to recreate that feeling/experience?

Prioritize The Experiences That Matter To You

One of an early home renovation project I worked on was for a young lady from the Bay area who had purchased a starter home on a hillside in a suburb. She didn't have a lot of money, so she bought a "fixer-upper" with a great view from the backyard. She used to live in the city, and in her previous home, she had an incredible view of the Bay Bridge from her living room. She reminisced about her last home and realized that she wanted to recreate the experience of living in a city. After a long day from work, she wanted to come home to her own sanctuary and relax and unwind by admiring the city lights sparkling.

Then I noticed there was a big mirror over the sink in her dark master suite on the second-floor — and the mirror was covering the very city view that she was longing for. It was a perfect opportunity to create the city living within her new suburban enclave, giving her the best of both worlds. She prioritized that city view over a chance to stare at herself in front of a mirror when she washes her hands.

So, we renovated her master suite, removed the mirror, and opened the wall to place a big window, giving her a breathtaking city view from her master bedroom. Because the opening was southwest-facing, it instantly brightened up the master suite during the daytime, and at night, she can drift off to sleep as the shimmering city lights dance on the walls. Not only did she gain an impressive city view, and a brighter master suite, she was able to significantly reduce her electric bill during the winter. It was a simple and affordable renovation that achieved an optimal outcome.

As you think about what things that you may want or can't live without, you may also consider your surroundings, such as how the sun moves through your home throughout the day. Studies have shown that natural light can have many positive benefits, affecting mental health, positively altering your mood, and helping to expedite recovery from illness. Of course, when your project is designed smartly, there are also significant benefits, such as lower energy consumption and a reduced carbon footprint. I always encourage incorporating sustainability into your design; it can save you loads of money on heating and cooling costs, it's good for you and the environment, and it's the socially responsible thing to do for our planet and for future generations. Plus, it makes you a brilliant and responsible homeowner — way to go! (Also, as previously mentioned, I went to Cal Berkeley, so it's second nature to me.) Fear not, we'll take a deeper dive into sustainability in another chapter — just you wait.

Along the same thought process, there are a few other factors to be mindful of during the design brainstorming phase:

- Passive cooling during summer
  - Landscaping/Vegetation (e.g., Are there trees or bushes to protect your home from harshest summer sun?)
  - Breezes/Wind direction (e.g., Where does the breeze come from?)
  - Shades (e.g., What is your summer sun path?)
- Passive heating during winter
  - Sunlight path (e.g., Where is your best winter sun exposure?)
- Views
  - Pleasant (e.g., Is there a view to maximize and enjoy?)
  - Unpleasant (e.g., Is there a view to minimize or avoid?)
- Privacy
  - Visual (e.g., Where do you need protection from public view into your space?)
  - Sound (e.g., Where do you need protection from unwanted noise invading your space?)

When you design a space with these factors in mind, you will be maximizing your investment and saving money in both the short and long term. These factors can increase the unexpected added value of your new and improved home, both financially and environmentally, and you'll reap the benefits for many years to come. You'll feel good about making such smart decisions, creating the home that upgrades your life.

Now you have some ideas about how to think through your design approach as you visualize your new space with more clarity. By taking a holistic approach to your design and factoring in your surroundings, you'll be more closely aligned with your **WHY** — but don't forget to connect your **WHY/FI** to double check everything.

"As an architect, you design for the present, with an awareness of the past, for a future which is essentially unknown."
- Norman Foster, Architect

"The future influences the present just as much as the past."
- Friedrich Nietzsche, Philosopher

Insider Tips

Designing a space is a lot like creating a delightful food dish. When you understand and appreciate the beauty and the essence of each ingredient in its measured quantity, you have a deeper understanding of how they all blend to create the delicious combinations of flavors and textures to excite your palette, creating a savory culinary masterpiece. It's the same with your home reno project; you're paying close attention to the ingredients and how they interact with one another to create the eye candy you want in your home. Visualize the space that you wanted to improve, then write down how the environmental factors impact the design. You might discover just how much flavor your home has!

MASTER PLAN

Space or Room	Environmental Factors	Desired Experience
Example: Kitchen	Northeast corner of the house. Shade and well-lighted. Ventilation with breeze from the westside.	Easy access to outdoor deck. Great central space to cook, host gatherings, do laundry and homework

6 Crawl Before You Run

We've already covered your hesitation and fears surrounding your home improvements. Here's some real talk: This project will likely cause you some anxiety, as well as some excitement. And that's okay. Congrats, you're human! While you can approach the problem logically, confronting the reasons for your fears head-on, don't be unrealistic and expect that you're going to eradicate all your fears at once. It's a marathon, not a sprint. So, be kind to yourself.

You know that old saying, "You need to crawl before you walk"? Well, many homeowners put undue pressure on themselves by trying to run before they even crawl. Don't do that to yourself. Rather than diving into the deep end and tackling a major home remodel that could cause you to nearly drowning in enormous stress and anxiety, consider taking on a single, smaller project to feel the rewards first. It's like getting in the shallow end and gradually walking toward the deeper end until your feet can no longer touch the bottom of the pool — but that's cool, 'cuz you can just tread water and keep your head above water for a bit until you're ready to swim to shore.

For example, it's unlikely that every room in your home is going to need a complete overhaul all at once. Sure, your kitchen may need an update, or you may be planning on adding on a family room addition. No doubt, these will go a long way toward making your home into the palace you've always dreamed of, but you don't need to tackle it all at once, even though you may want to try.

Priming the Pump

Jim and Linda live in a tiny home that desperately needs an overhaul. The furnishings are outdated. They're planning a significant addition with a new family room and kitchen, but they're a little nervous about the beginning. How will they live through the chaos? Can they really trust their designer or contractor and each other to work together toward this goal?

They decide to do a test run and break the big project down into multiple phases, choosing to focus on their living room. This baby step represents an achievable goal, they will have a space to live in while the major remodel is going on, and it lets them test the waters of a major project.

They have their living room repainted, new flooring put in, and custom bookcases built. The room becomes lighter, appears larger, and is much more functional and less cluttered with the built-in storage. Jim and Linda are thrilled with the results and are now actively looking forward to their new family room addition as well.

This scenario is known as "priming the pump." It helps give nervous homeowners a chance to get their feet wet and work through any anxiety they may have by tackling a smaller project. Better yet, they get an immediate sense of satisfaction that they can recall and build from as they take on larger projects.

Don't get it twisted: at first, it might seem like you're avoiding the bigger project or procrastinating. To the contrary — you're actually preparing yourself for it, but you're strategic about it. By racking up some smaller victories, you'll be able to learn from the process, collect and evaluate the feedback, and savor the feeling of satisfaction and the sense of reward that come from completing a project.

If the idea of a full-scale remodel is scary, consider starting with something small, like Jim and Linda's living room makeover so you can get into to renovation groove more gradually, get a taste of what to expect from the process, and learn from the experience.

By taking this approach, Jim and Linda learned that they could trust their designer and contractor. They learned to communicate and make decisions together on simple things like wall color and flooring, which aren't quite as scary as more critical decisions such as ceiling heights and the number of windows. And they also learned to appreciate and love their home a little bit more than they did before they began. Once they could see the actual results of what they'd started, they immediately wanted to continue. The experience they gained from the living room makeover gave them the confidence they needed to begin their full-scale renovation.

So, if you find yourself nervous about beginning a major project, stop and take a deep breath. Check yourself before you wreck yourself. Just prime the pump a little. Instead of diving headlong into a full-on kitchen remodel, start with some smaller projects. Consider installing new lighting in your bedroom, or putting in a new entryway floor. Once you manage to confront some of your fears in a smaller, more practical way, they tend to fade away, paving the way for the bigger projects to follow.

Remember, CRAWL BEFORE YOU RUN. (It's the title of this chapter for a reason.) Focus on crawling first, then walking, then eventually, running with the proverbial big dogs. You'll set yourself up for success by being strategic. That's called being smart. You don't just decide to run a marathon; you start by training for it, getting your stamina up, and running 5K and then 10K runs. This prevents injury, and you get a sense of accomplishment from the incremental victories.

Here's another way to think about it: You don't just start by headlining Coachella on both weekends. Not even Beyoncé did that! You start by performing in smaller venues and stages, getting a feel for what works as you build your act. As you get better and

stronger, you move up to bigger stages. Do you see where we're going with this analogy? Much like Jim and Linda, even Queen B had to crawl before she could run.

"It takes as much energy to wish as it does to plan."
\- Eleanor Roosevelt, FLOTUS

Insider Tips

Your home is an extension of who you are and what you stand for. Your home can have a significant direct emotional impact on your life. Consider how much time you spend in your home, creating memories with people that matter most to you. You don't have to compromise or settle for less. You deserve to live in a home that positively reflects who you are. Planning is necessary to keep good control of any project, and it is one of the most powerful and effective ways to attain what you want. Nobody plans to fail; they just fail to plan. Let's build your home improvement game plan. A goal without a plan is just a wish, so let's set a plan to accomplish your goals. Start with your Improvement Goals, and let's identify your upgrade goals.

HOME IMPROVEMENT GAME PLAN

Improvement Goals	Target Start	Target Completion
Example: New big and open kitchen to accommodate everyday usage meal preparation, and large gatherings. Want to achieve timeless design while easy to maintain throughout the year.	September	November

7 Trust Your Gut
Just Do You

We've talked about the most common concerns and fears related to home improvements: money/budget constraints, trusting Pros, the inconvenience, and fear of the unknown. But there's another fear that you might have, but may not be comfortable acknowledging — the uncertainty of what to do to your home.

Take a quick scroll through Pinterest, Houzz, and Instagram, or flip through the pages of any home décor-based magazine and you'll see countless images of beautiful homes. You'll see fixtures, furnishings, surfaces, and colors you like, no doubt. These images are inspirational ... aspirational, even; that's what they're intended to be. Often, they bring to mind more questions than answers. Which one is right for you, your lifestyle, and your home? Will the same type of renovation work with your space? How can you be sure? These questions often stump people, because while they think something may be beautiful, how can they be sure it's the right choice for their home?

Before you let these questions shut you down, remember this: there isn't one right answer. At the end of the day, it's up to YOU to decide. There are many different styles, colors, and themes that can complement a home, just as there are many materials and ways to achieve a look. If an image resonates with you, take a moment to consider why. Is it the color? The space layout? The ceiling height?

The finishes? The hardware? That surfaces? Next, try to envision this look in your space. Can you see the finished product? Your instincts are the reason it caught your attention in the first place. Something said to you, "THIS would look great in your home!" Your instincts recognized something that fit within color and design preferences, that's why they spoke up via that internal voice. Listen to your instincts, let them guide you.

Trends vs. Fads

Many people worry about choosing something "trendy" for their homes. They worry that if they choose something trendy that it will go out of style quickly and their home look dated. They also worry that if they don't choose something "on trend" that it could make their home more difficult to sell.

First, consider trends versus fads. A trend is actually something popular that lasts for several years. Granite countertops, for example. However, a fad is something that only lasts a short period of time. Its popularity flares up and burns bright for a brief period of time, then flames out, as another fad takes its place. Tumbled marble backsplashes in the early aughts were a fad. (So were velvet chokers, slouch socks, and henna tattoos. That doesn't mean you'd want to wear them for years to come. Apply this thinking to your home.)

Therefore, the first thing you need to do when wondering whether or not to include something trendy is to RELAX.

It's not a crime to consider trends, but you need to make sure it's something that you really love for the right reasons, not just because it's on trend. Do a little homework and examine what this trend is and how long it's been around. Do you see other examples of it as you look through images for inspiration? If the trend is brand new, it might be a good idea to wait a bit and see how the trend develops before including it in your design to make sure it's an actual trend. If it's already been around for a while, this indicates a lasting trend that can be a great thing to add to your home. If you plan on selling your home within the next 10 years, be careful not to select any trend that might be tapering off, making it more challenging to sell. Be realistic and be practical.

Trusting Yourself

Unless you are remodeling your home to flip it and make some cash, you're going to be the one who feels the biggest, most immediate impact from the choices you make — not the next tenants who live there. You need to ask yourself if the choices you are making are going to make you happy in your home. Will they bring you joy as you cook in your new kitchen? While you soak in the tub in your newly upgraded bathroom, will you feel a sense of fulfillment? Will these choices improve your home, make your life easier, and better meet your needs? Are they going to allow you and your family to use your home more efficiently?

If the answer to these questions is yes, then you need to trust those instincts and that you are making the right decision for your home. Heck, even if you plan on selling your home in five years, it's still okay to trust yourself. Because making good decisions for your home and its design doesn't always mean just following trends. Sometimes, it means making decisions that are best for the home and how you live in it. Anyone, even the next family who lives there, can appreciate that, even if they hate your wall colors and decide to repaint.

Just be sure to keep the fads to a minimum. If you really like a current fad, it's okay to incorporate it into your space -- just be smart about it and do it in a way that won't require a major renovation to correct. Throw pillows, linens, and other decors are great ways to embrace a fad. When the fad is over, you can just donate those items and remove them from the space -- no need to tear down a wall or reroute plumbing. If you love a particular color or material, use restraint. Keep them contained to small areas, like backsplashes or wall colors that can be easily changed. That way, you can indulge yourself and embrace the trend without worrying about affecting resale later on.

Bottom Line: It's YOUR Home, You Know Best

If you already live in a home, then you know that space better than anyone else — even your Pro. That means that you can make better decisions for that space than someone who doesn't live there, and who doesn't have to care for and interact the space once it's done. It's your space, your sanctuary. Make choices that you will love and enjoy for years to come. Don't let fads dictate your decor. Trust your instincts and JUST DO YOU.

"Be yourself; everyone else is already taken."
— Oscar Wilde, Poet

"We can achieve what we can conceive and believe."
- Mark Twain, Author

Insider Tips

Thinking about the final destination of your home improvement journey will help you to ease into the process. What will the new space feel like? What will it look like? As you define your vision of the new space, you can use the worksheet below to collect the information. So by the time you're ready to kick off the project, you'll be ahead of the game, and it will help your Pro to see your vision.

Do what you love and just do you. Others may have opinions and suggestions. Ultimately, you know your space and how you want to live in it better than anybody else. Don't get overwhelmed; just take one step at a time, and break out the project into bite-sized tasks.

JUST DO YOU WORKSHEET

I Want/Need	... and It Will Make Me Feel
Example: *When I get out of shower, I want to have warm towels to dry up in my bathroom.*	*Having a warm towel after a shower will make me feel like in a spa — relaxed and warm. And I will also feel smart because I will put my towel back to dry after I'm done. It will also conserve water since I don't need to wash it frequently.*

PART II

Set

8   For the Love of It

Up to this point, we've talked about fear. A lot. There's always a method to the madness; fear is a necessary part of the process, but it shouldn't <u>drive</u> the process. Enough with all the doom and gloom -- let's talk about how you can transform those fears into the dream home that you'll LOVE.

Think of your dreams. What do you envision when you think of your ideal home? Close your eyes ... now what do you see? A dream kitchen suitable for a world-class chef? A luxury living room designed for entertaining? Or, perhaps a master bedroom suite that makes you feel like your home really is your castle?

Your dreams are not rooted in reality; they're amorphous, and they constantly shift to fit your mood or the current state of mind. However, you have tools at your disposal to help turn those dreams into reality. So, let's start there and begin with the end in mind.

Now, prepare to translate your dreams into goals. Break them down component by component and determine what it is about each thing that you LOVE. Why does it appeal to you? In what ways is the dream different from your current reality? Focus on that facet and make that mini dream into a major goal.

For example, let's say you're dreaming about your dream kitchen. It's bright, sleek, modern, and has plenty of surfaces to prepare a feast for your nearest and dearest. However, your current reality is that your kitchen is very closed off, more cabinets than there are surfaces, and two people can barely fit in it. That's your living nightmare -- and your starting point.

Begin with the layout that doesn't flow. As you plan your renovation, make the layout your starting point so you can ensure that your new kitchen will give you plenty of space to move, prepare, and converse with friends and family. GOAL! Next, take those cabinets that currently make you feel closed in and vow to replace them with smarter storage options that don't box you in. Another goal!

As you break down your dreams, you'll find you're making a checklist of your wants and needs. Whether you're renovating to increase resale value or upgrading to your dream space for years to come, you're drawing the roadmap for your renovation! You're focusing on specific characteristics of your home that you want to improve and/or transform, and you're doing it strategically.

Get Practical

Remember, we're talking about taking your dreams and translating them into goals, so remember this mission imperative as you move through them: BE PRACTICAL. Now, that might sound like the exact opposite of what you want to achieve with this exercise, but hear me out. I want you to break your dreams down and use that as the basis for the transformations you want to make, but I also want you to look at realistic, practical solutions. It's likely that your dreams are your subconscious looking for a way to solve a real-world problem.

The home of your dreams might be an over-the-top luxury, high technology, sleek design, and perfection -- just like you might see in a movie. But here's a spoiler alert: those perfect, high tech rooms in movies aren't functional -- they just need to look good on camera. Sure, they look amazing on screen, but on the other side, you'll see they are made of plywood and materials that would never withstand even a normal day of practical use in your real-life. It's smoke and mirrors. Your job is to determine the practical solution that is as close to your dream as your timeline and budget will allow.

Take a moment to examine each dream. What is the problem with the current situation that you'd like to resolve? What is your subconscious dreaming mind trying to tell you? Once you have identified the problem, you can ask yourself this question: "What will the best solution be?"

Remember the Love!

As you consider possible solutions, you should include things that you genuinely love. Things that will not only improve your home but will also bring you joy for years to come. You need to see the problems clearly to see the solutions. Sometimes, that thing you absolutely love will be your inspiration and starting point.

For every room that you remodel, ask yourself, "What is the one thing that I most want to see in that space?" — And then make that the centerpiece for each renovation. Whether it's a towel warmer in the bathroom, a picture window in the living room, or an island in the kitchen, make sure you make that the most essential feature, and you may find that helps drive clarity for the rest of the design. Using this idea as the driving force will keep you going through the whole renovation.

Once you identify the one aspect that you're dying to see incorporated, it's easier to look at the rest of the space and see what you need to do to get there. For example, if that towel warmer is the goal for the bathroom, then you need to make sure you have the space set up for it, which may mean changing the layout. While you change the layout, you can think about how best to use the rest of the space. Heck, you might even discover a new configuration that makes better use of the space and improves your life even more!

You Do You

Unless you are flipping the home, remember that you're remodeling for YOU. You're creating your dream home. If achieving your goal and staying on a budget means you need to make concessions in other areas, then you can do that without sacrificing the thing that will make you happiest when the project is done. It's the one facet that you'll love long after the tarps, sawdust, hammering, and reno mess is gone. You want to look at it every day and think, "Damn, I'm glad I made this a priority, 'cuz it makes this feel more like home. MY home. It was all worth it." (You might even say it in an accent, depending on what your inner voice sounds like. Mine sounds like Helen Mirren.)

Comparison Is The Thief Of Joy - Don't Be A Joy Thief!

It's human nature to compare yourself to others. With the advent of social media, it's easier than ever to scroll through and see other people who appear to have everything fabulous and see how you measure up. It's okay, everyone does it ... just make sure you're doing it for the right reasons. We tend to look at others -- how they look, what they have, what they drive, the house they live in, the clothes they wear, their relationships -- and then look at ourselves to see how we measure up. More often than not, this ends up in disappointment or feelings of inadequacy. Why would you do that to yourself? There's a reason they say, "Comparison is the thief of joy." It's time to reprogram your brain and stop being a joy thief!

We're not saying you should never compare yourself or your home to others; just be smart about it. A comparison should be used for inspirational and aspirational purposes. Let's say your carpet is outdated and stained. You're much more likely to notice the gleaming new hardwood flooring in your friend's house. Don't let it make you feel less than. Instead, let it inspire you to choose something that will impact and improve your life, but choose an option that YOU like.

If your home isn't quite what you want it to be, you may find yourself hyper-aware of other homes around you, and you jump to comparison because that's how you're wired. Instead of letting it make you feel inferior because it's newer, prettier, or more expensive than yours, stop that negativity in its tracks and turn it around into more inspiration to make your home uniquely YOURS!

Comparison of inspiration is the name of the game, but one of the main rules of that game is to make sure it's a fair comparison. You can't watch an episode of *Bazillion Dollar Mansions* and compare the living room in a 30,000 square foot house on the cliffs of Malibu to your quaint home. That's not a fair comparison ... unless you are Candy Spelling. (Which you probably aren't, because she has no need for this book -- she has a freakin' gift wrapping room the size of an NYC duplex ... but I digress.)

That gleaming, pristine marble entryway your neighbors with no kids and no pets just installed? Sure it looks fantastic, and you love the look, but is it really right for your home? You have children who play sports and two dogs, so that beautiful new marble won't be beautiful for long, thanks to dog claws, soccer cleats, and all that gear. It's probably not the best option for you, but let it inspire you. Start thinking about what you like about it, then consider available options that could deliver a comparable look and feel that's better suited to your lifestyle. You'll end up with a cleaner, more durable flooring option that will enhance your life and improve YOUR home. Remember that part about being practical in the previous chapter? Boom — mic drop! (Well, if you're practical, maybe just gently set the mic down on the ground.)

Inspiration, Not Comparison

You'll find yourself a lot happier with the entire home improvement process if you start looking at other people's homes as inspiration, rather than as a comparison to yours. Let those beautiful visuals help get you excited about the transformation your home is about to undergo, but don't let them trap you into something that isn't right for you.

"You can't control how other people see you or think of you. But you have to be comfortable with that."
- Helen Mirren, Actor

Insider Tips

Most of us are really busy and don't like to clean. So, selecting the right finishing material for your home can save your time, money, and reduce stress & avoid headaches. Unless you have a daily cleaning crew who perform deep cleaning throughout your home, you'll be better off by keeping it simple and doing some homework before you commit to buy. You may visit a showroom to get a full-size sample and test it out; ask a child to draw on it with crayon, spill red wine, or smear dirt on it. Put it to the real-world durability test. Have fun!

FORESIGHT MAGIC 8 BALL WORKSHEET

Finishing Material	Desired Outcome	Maintenance Effort (High, Medium, Low)	Alternative Options
Example: Marble floor tiles at the entrance	Classy, grand	H	Porcelain or stained concrete (resemble polished marble) or outsourcing cleaning

9 Sustainability is Sexy

These days, there's a big emphasis being placed on sustainability when it comes to the home. From the rising costs of energy to a need to be more conscious about the choices being made for materials in the home, many homeowners starting a home renovation project are taking the time to consider sustainable (energy efficient) design and use the Eco-friendly material. You hear buzzwords such as, sustainable design, energy efficient design, green building design, and the Eco-friendly design ... but what do these terms mean? While they're related and often used interchangeably, the four terms actually mean slightly different things, and — depending on your personal goals — may also change how you approach your renovation.

Sustainability

Sustainable design is the philosophy of meets the current needs without compromising the ability of future generations to meet their own needs, e.g., minimize waste, reduce consumption of non-renewable resources, increase renewable energy, use green & eco-friendly building materials, and protect and conserve water. What most people think of when they consider green building is sustainability, which means that the project has the least amount of impact on the environment, or that it's sustainable regarding long-term environmental impact. This impacts areas such as the use of green building materials and committing to the Eco-friendly designs. Let's break down these categories:

Efficiency

The most efficient homes are the ones that use the least amount of energy and resources. Efficiency can mean using appliances specifically designed to use less energy, or it can mean properly sealing and insulating your home so that less efficient appliances don't have to work as hard, e.g., use Energy Star appliances. Water use sometimes falls under the umbrella of efficiency. Water can be managed in two ways: through the use of water-saving appliances, and through the recycling of "greywater" or water used first for things like dishes and laundry, that is then repurposed for watering the lawn or landscaping. In recent years, the collection and harvesting of rainwater have gained popularity, especially for purposes ranging from cleaning, irrigation, and lawn care, to the purification allowing it to be used for cooking and drinking.

Renewable Energy

Renewable energy sources include solar and wind power. Equipping your home to capture and leverage these sources can be one of the smartest investments in your home that you can make. Homeowners typically see tremendous returns on such investments in the form of thousands of dollars saved annually. Take out your latest utility statements and crunch some numbers; you might be surprised at how much you're paying, and how much you could save by investing in renewable energy. Simple improvements such as solar panels or shingles for your home could also earn you a rebate or tax credit, depending on your state or local regulations and incentives. I'm just sayin'.

Green Building

Green design reduces the footprint it leaves on the natural environment and on the health of its current inhabitants. This term often refers to materials. For example, a more environmentally friendly material such as fiber cement gives off fewer VOCs (Volatile Organic Compounds) in manufacturing, or vinyl, which requires less maintenance and waste, compared to wood.

Eco-Friendly

Eco-friendly (or earth-friendly or not harmful to the environment) means the design is using local building materials, local techniques, and also are low cost, e.g., products with "made from recycled materials" contain glass, wood, metal or plastic reclaimed from waste products and made into something new. Biodegradable products break down through natural decomposition, which is less taxing on landfills and the ecosystem as a whole. In addition to the eco-friendly materials, you've probably heard the term "reclaimed" used with increasing frequency. Reclaimed (also called reused or salvaged) items can include not only things like lumber and wood flooring, but also reclaimed architectural features such as moldings, mantels, clawfoot tubs, pedestal sinks, and even cabinetry, that are repurposed from older buildings and placed into new ones. Using reclaimed items mean less waste from tear-outs, as well as less of an environmental impact from production issues. Plus, it can also add unique aesthetic touches that elevate and REVIVIFY your renovation. (I'll bet you didn't think I could work part of the book title into this section, did you? Let's call it another example of reclaimed material!)

Creating An Efficient Home

One part of an Eco-friendly design and a home that is resource-efficient is creating a home or building that uses less energy, which is an attractive option for most homeowners. Studies have shown that for every dollar you spend on home improvements to increase the energy efficiency of your home, you'll save seven dollars on your energy bills. That's a 700% ROI (Return On Investment)! If you're already having work done on your home, it makes sense to upgrade your energy efficiency at the same time. In fact, I'd dare say it's a no-brainer. To quote Nike, JUST DO IT.

Insulate Yourself!

The vast majority of homes, particularly those built before the 1960s, are insufficiently insulated, meaning that they don't have enough insulation in the attic, walls, or exterior. Adding insulation to your attic, the underside of your roof deck, your exterior beneath your siding, and inside your walls can severely impact how comfortable your home is, and how well it performs. Best of all, adding attic insulation will recoup you a whopping 113% of the cost at the time of resale. (In case you needed incentive.)

Mind The Gap!

Did you know that if you have a poor air seal around your windows and doors, you could be losing as much as 40% of the energy you use to heat and cool your home? That's effectively throwing money into the trash. Poor air seal is one of the biggest problems most homeowners face, and they don't even know it. Sealing up this gap will make the biggest immediate impact on your energy bills — and your bank account. As they say when waiting for the London Underground … MIND THE GAP!

Fixing Your Chimney

If you have a fireplace, you could be losing about 20% of the energy you use to heat and cool that room right up to it. Why? Because most chimney dampers aren't installed correctly or don't fit quite right. So all the warm and cool air you pump in flies right up, even with the flue is shut. Fix your chimney to make that room more comfortable year round ... it's not just something to think about on Christmas Eve.

Attic Ventilation

Attic vents are another area that most homeowners are unintentionally overlooking. Attic vents remove excess heat from your attic year round. In the summer, this prevents your attic and roof from overheating, because less heat gets transferred down to your living spaces. This means that your home stays cooler longer, with less money out of your pocket.

Getting Into Hot Water - Replace Your Hot Water Tank

Make this one a hot-button priority! Of all the different energy saving appliances out there, the hot water tank is the one to replace first. Old hot water tanks use significantly more energy to heat your water than newer models. If you aren't attached to the idea of a tank, consider moving to a tankless model, which heats water as you need it, will save you even more moolah!

HVAC System

Your HVAC system is another area that could be draining your home of energy each month. There are several issues here:

- Older systems are much less energy-efficient than newer models — if yours is more than 10 years old, consider upgrading
- Many homes have systems that are too large for the space, which means they use more energy than they actually require — this is *literally* blowing money away
- Old or dirty ductwork could lose as much as 20% of the energy you use to heat your home as it travels through the house

- Not performing regular maintenance could mean that your HVAC is working harder than it needs to, resulting in more energy usage

Replacing your current HVAC system with a newer, more energy efficient model that is appropriately sized for your home will save you hundreds each year, at a minimum.

Smart Thermostat

Thermostats today do more than controlling the temperature of the room; they also learn your patterns and will shut themselves off when you're away. Investing in a smart thermostat will give you greater control over the energy you use each day, saving you money you didn't know you were wasting. Some models are even controlled by an app, which means you can monitor and adjust your smart thermostat from your smartphone!

Radiant Heat Mats

If you're replacing the flooring anywhere in your home, consider putting in a radiant heat mat. Each mat only uses roughly the same amount of electricity as a light bulb but will make your room feel much warmer and more comfortable than your current system. This is because the mat heats you, and your furnishings, but not the air. So there's less wasted heat and less wasted energy.

Energy Star Appliances

If you plan on remodeling your kitchen, make sure you opt for Energy Star-rated appliances, which can save you money each month that you run them. Look for models that use not only less energy, but less water as well to save even more.

Water Saving Appliances

A lot of people think of heating, cooling, and electricity and over-look their water usage. Investing in water saving appliances, such as low-flush toilets and water restricting faucets and showerheads will save you thousands of gallons of water every year. New technologies mean that you won't even notice a drop in performance at the same time.

Choosing the Eco-Friendly Green Building Materials

The other side of the Eco-friendly home improvements comes from selecting materials that are green or the Eco-friendly as your choices throughout the home. In most cases, there are greener options for everything from your faucets to your flooring, with many of them at or around the same cost as the non-green materials. Best of all, you can go green without having to compromise style, comfort, utility, or durability! Some choices you may want to consider as part of your home improvements include:

- Recycled glass tile or countertops
- Wood flooring from a company that practices the Eco-friendly manufacturing
- Reclaimed stone, tile, or wood from older homes and buildings
- Porcelain tile made from recycled clay

Green Bathroom

One of the most common improvement projects is the bathroom. There are a lot of simple things you can do that will make a world of difference. Here are some green bathroom production options to consider:

Towel Warmers

Most people think of towel warmers as a luxury or something that only the rich install in their bathrooms — on their private jets. However, recent studies have found that towel warmers actually save thousands of gallons of water a year in the laundry. How? By keeping your towels drier, so they stay fresher longer, and require less frequent washings. Think of it this way, it's recommended that you wash your bath towels three times a week, and your hand towels twice a week. That's about 320 gallons of water a week just in towel washings. With a towel warmer, because your towels will be less susceptible to mildew spores, you can eliminate one washing a week, saving thousands of gallons of water a year. Best of all, you can have warm, fluffy, dry towels every single day for about the same amount of electricity that it takes to run a light bulb. Wrap yourself up in that fact!

Put A Cork In It: Cork Flooring

Looking for a trendy, sustainable, and attractive flooring option that's also water-resistant, anti-microbial, and feels good enough underfoot to reduce fatigue when standing on it? Look no further than cork. You're probably thinking of that porous material that comes in your wine bottles, or maybe something you use to keep track of notes and memos. Well, put a pin in that, because cork is actually a beautiful, sustainable flooring choice that comes in many different colors, sizes, and patterns. It's made from the bark of a tree that can be harvested without killing or harming the tree itself, which makes it super the Eco-friendly. Plus, cork floor tiles are lightweight and springy; they feel great underfoot and can be beneficial to those with problems in their feet, legs, or backs.

Formaldehyde Free Cabinets

Formaldehyde in your cabinets?! Yes, that's right — the very cabinets where you store your food and dishes likely contain formaldehyde, which is given off, along with other VOCs (Volatile Organic Compounds) into the air you breathe. This is not only bad for the environment, but it's also bad for your health, particularly if you're sensitive to chemicals. Be sure to inquire about formaldehyde-free options, as more plywood manufacturers are switching to a formaldehyde-free construction, which gives off little to no VOCs. Your cabinets will look just as beautiful, and you can breathe easy without breathing in harmful chemicals. Talk about a breath of fresh air!

Time to Go Tankless

You probably don't give much thought to your water heater … until it stops working. While you're not thinking of it, it's down in your basement, quietly eating up energy doing nothing more than maintaining the temperature of the water inside. So, while you're at work all day, making money, your water heater is sitting there wasting it, consuming energy.

Tankless water heaters work differently; they only heat the water as you use it, so they use a lot less energy. Newer models have eliminated the "cold water sandwich" of older designs, plus the heater itself takes up very little space in your walls. No more giant tank in your basement, which will slowly fill with sediment, reducing your water quality. Now you have more space, better quality water, and lower energy bills all at once.

You'll Feel Absolutely Radiant

You've probably seen those electric mats so popular for bathroom floors. They warm the floor of your bathroom, so you never have to step on cold tile. But did you know that these mats can actually heat a lot more than just your bathroom? Radiant heat is the most efficient way to warm your home. Instead of heating the air, it warms only the people and objects that touch it directly. So, you and your furnishings will be warm, but the air won't be. This takes a fraction of the amount of energy that forced hot air or water does to make you feel the same level of toasty. Best of all, radiant heat will maintain your room at a constant, even temperature. No more cool spots or plummeting temperatures before the thermostat kicks back on ... just constant, soothing warmth.

Green Kitchen

The kitchen is one of the most frequently updated and renovated rooms in the home, since it's one of the most commonly used rooms, that you likely visit every day. It's the heart of your home. People gather in the kitchen, cook, eat, hang out, and entertain there. As the old saying goes, "No matter where I serve my guests, it seems they like my kitchen best." Chances are, if you're planning any type of home renovation, you're likely to include the kitchen in your plans. Given the amount of time you spend there and the type of functions this space preforms, it also makes sense that you'll want to include some green building practices in your kitchen remodel.

What It Means to Have a Green Kitchen

The kitchen is a unique space in the home. You don't just hang out and gather there, you also prepare food there, clean things there, and eat there. So when you're designing a green kitchen, you need to come at it from a few different angles.

First, let's think about energy usage. Kitchens use a lot of energy on a daily basis. Cooking, cleaning, food storage, and illumination all take some degree of electricity and water usage. So at a minimum, your green kitchen design should include some energy efficient appliances and faucets.

But the kitchen is more than a functional place; it's also where you go to gather and eat. With food being kept, stored, cooked, and eaten here, you want to keep the VOCs to a minimum whenever possible. For this reason, you'll want to look into things like urea formaldehyde-free plywood for your kitchen cabinets.

Finally, you'll also want to consider the surface materials of your countertops/. Kitchens have a lot of hardwood, stone, tile, and glass built right into them. With the counters, cabinets, shelves, and other surfaces, your kitchen may need more attention and more building materials than any other room in the home. You have more opportunities to select sustainable materials for your kitchen than in any other room in your home, so it's easy to go green!

Bamboo lumber, formaldehyde-free cabinetry, and counter-tops made of recycled glass are all excellent places to start. There are many options that have little to no VOCs and are made from a high percentage of recycled content — and don't forget to look into reclaimed options that may be available.

A truly green kitchen takes from all of these areas of sustain-ability, not just one or two. It's fine to have a recycled glass counter if that's what you like, but to install only this and not to pay atten-tion to the rest of the design does not a green kitchen make. Take a holistic approach and give careful thought to each area to ensure that the area where you store, prepare, and consume the food that nourishes your body is as green and healthy as possible.

Should You Go Green in the Kitchen?

As Kermit the Frog might say, "It ain't easy being green." Green building practices often take a slight more time and effort to pull together. You need to research each material, compare it with oth-ers, and make your final choice based both on its sustainability and on how well it works with the rest of the design. So is it worth it?

Given the amount of use the kitchen gets and how much time you spend there, the answer to that question is a resounding YES. Installing LED light fixtures, energy saving appliances, and water-friendly features in the kitchen means that you'll save money each month on your energy bills. Choosing low VOC paint and

flooring, and making sure that your cabinets are free of formaldehyde will ensure that your kitchen is safer for you and the food you prepare there. The Eco-friendly design can also have a positive impact on your home's resale value, as well as on how quickly it sells when the time comes.

Creating a Greener and Sustainable Home

When it comes to creating a more sustainable design for your home, you can include any of the above areas; sustainability is not an all or nothing proposition. For some people, creating the greenest home possible is the goal, while others may just want to reduce energy consumption and bills each month. Consider what sustainability means to you and how far you want to take it in your home to get the most workable solution for you and your family.

> *"The natural environment sustains the life of all beings universally."*
> — His Holiness the Dalai Lama, Spiritual Leader

Insider Tips

Saving energy can also save you money both short-term (like instant rebates and tax credits), and long-term (like reduction of your monthly energy bill). There are many great resources to help you get inspired on sustainability ideas and provide the rebate information to help you save money. As you define the scope of your project, you can have qualified residential energy professionals, or you can also follow the DIY audit guide by Home Energy Saver energy calculator to figure out the savings for the improvements that you plan to implement. You can also check out some of these resources to get ideas: Energy.gov for rebate information, download their Energy Saver Guide for more helpful tips; and Green Architecture and Building Report to see how other people have incorporated sustainable products in their home around the world.

Sustainable Options Worksheet

Issue	Options	Rebates/Credit
Example: *High Electric Bill*	*Replace/Add:* *- Windows* *- Programmable Thermostat* *- High efficiency, Energy Star rated HVAC* *- Eco-Friendly LED Lights* *- Insulations with high R rating* *- Tankless Water Heaters*	

10   Make It Happen

If you're anything like me, there have been countless occasions when you've found yourself in situations that are unpleasant or even seemingly unbearable. You have two ways of approaching these situations: you either accept that the situation must go forward, so you make every attempt to grin and bear it in good humor, or you attempt to just get it over with quickly, enduring it and cursing the situation the entire time. The outcome is usually the same, but the way that you approach it can often mean the difference between being miserable and potentially enjoying yourself. Which option would you choose? Oh, yeah ... in case you didn't realize it, you DO have a choice, because attitude and mindset are everything. When you change your mindset, your attitude will follow.

Imagine you're a homeowner embarking on a new kitchen project. You might not be ready for this project, but you've discovered a water leak in your walls, leading to the spread of dangerous mold growth. You have no choice but to address this immediately. The clock is ticking, and it's time to take action. This situation is indeed not ideal, but it's a very common one that plays out on a regular basis.

Now, let's imagine that you only see the inconvenience. You'll be without a kitchen for months. Insurance is paying for it, but there's a lot of red tapes and endless expenses that it doesn't cover, such as takeout food while you're without a kitchen.

The entire process is stressful, full of headaches, and you just wish it would go away. When the kitchen is finally completed, you swear you'll never go through anything like it again, and you fail to notice that your new kitchen is more modern, cleaner, lighter, and more efficient than the old one. What would happen if you had a different attitude?

Now, let's imagine that you choose to look at this obstacle as an opportunity. You can finally get your dream kitchen, and better yet, the bulk of the cost is being paid for by the insurance company! Sure, it's inconvenient, and you'll have to explore takeout or pre-packaged meal service options for food, but in the end, you will have your new kitchen! Even better, it's going to be beautiful with all the new flooring, counters, and appliances you've dreamed of for years. When it's finally complete, you can't help but take a look at your new dream kitchen and smile with pride, because you weathered the storm, and turned an obstacle into an opportunity to show how unstoppable you are.

In both cases, the outcome was exactly the same. The only difference was in how you approached it. Home improvement comes with a certain amount of inconvenience, but it can also be fun, exciting, and fulfilling; it's all about how you choose to approach it.

Change the Way You Think

Rather than just viewing your home improvements as a hassle, significant expense, and serious inconvenience, try seeing them as opportunities to create your dream home. Opportunities are easier to embrace if you have the right attitude.

You don't need to create a fantasy world; it's better to stay grounded in reality. Yes, home improvements are messy, inconvenient and expensive, but the outcome is worth it. You should acknowledge these facts, but don't dwell on them. Instead, focus on the things that will make this situation into something wonderful — the end result of your beautiful new home, and the positive impact it will have on your life. Sure, there will be hurdles along the way, but the end result far outweighs them, so take a deep breath, adjust your attitude, and keep your eyes on the prize!

"The greatest discovery of all time is that a person can change his future by merely changing his attitude."
- Oprah Winfrey, Media Mogul,
Spiritual Guru, Ultimate Badass Boss

Smart Planning Equals Smart Savings

No matter how big or small your project, the cost of home improvements is bound to be a considerable amount. *(If money is not an issue for you, then please enjoy the next chapter.)* While some costs are unavoidable, strategically planning the project can result in significant savings. Remember, no matter what your budget is for this project, it's possible to both stay within it and still enjoy the finished results.

Timing Is Everything

That heading says it all. By knowing the best times to begin a project, book your Pros, or purchase your materials, you can get your project off the ground faster, and for less money. This is because the majority of people tend to schedule similar projects around the same time. By planning your project well ahead of time, and going with a different schedule than the one that most homeowners are following, you can help get your project off to a better start.

We all have that one friend who stocks up on wrapping paper

and holiday decorations during the first week of January. We might roll our eyes, but the joke's on us because she's planning way ahead and is scoring huge discounts on seasonal items when retailers are trying to unload their remaining stock, and the rest of us don't even want to think about anything holiday-related for another ten months.

Why Seasons Affect Home Improvement Projects

The spring and the fall are the two busiest times of year for home improvement projects. This is because many homeowners are influenced by things like culture, advertising, and subtle forms of peer pressure to get things done on a set schedule.

For example, when the weather begins to warm up in the spring, you'll start seeing multiple advertisements by big box stores telling you it's time to start working on your deck, landscaping, and patio. A quick look around your neighborhood will find your neighbors doing the same thing, which might help inspire you to take on jobs surrounding the exterior of your home, from fixing up problems caused by winter — leaking roofs or foundations — to sprucing up your home's curb appeal.

The same is true in the fall when many people begin to focus on their home's interior for the winter ahead and the guests coming to visit for the holidays. This all adds up to an imbalance in the home improvement trades. (You didn't even realize you were peer pressured, did you?)

Off-Season Can Be On Point

You're probably wondering what's wrong with following the same schedule as everyone else. It's human nature to want to go along with the rest of the herd. But unless you need to have work done — due to damage or are an urgent need for a repair — waiting can be to your advantage.

Pros that do specific types of work, like roofing and siding contractors, are in high demand during their on the season. This means that you may have to wait weeks just to get an estimate and be put on their schedule. This also means that you have less bargaining room on the price and that you may not even be able to get the Pro you really want.

Likewise, materials suppliers will be charging top dollar during high demand. It doesn't make sense for suppliers to hold sales during these times of the year; everyone is purchasing anyway. It's simple supply and demand, and they're trying to turn a profit.

By waiting until off-season — having your roofing and exterior work done in the fall, or your interior work done in the summer — you can often have Pros competing for your job, plus you'll find sales on the same materials that would have cost you a lot more at the peak times. (Just ask your friend how much she paid for that beautiful wrapping paper she bought on January 2nd.)

It's Always The Season For Savings /
The Best Times of Year to Complete a Project

Home improvements aren't entered into lightly. Chances are if you're having work done on your home, this is something you've been thinking about for a while. Did you know that when you're considering having something done, most other people are considering something similar at the same time? This can drive up your costs and make it harder to get the Pros that you want for your job. If you can time your project during the off-season, it might even go more quickly and end up costing you less. There's a basic timetable that just about all homeowners follow when it comes to having work done on their home. Do you want to stay with the herd? Or would you rather be the leader of the pack? Ditch the herd mentality and blaze a new trail on a new timeline!

Spring

Spring is a season of renewal and one of the busiest times of year for home improvements. Coming out of a long winter often puts people in the frame of mind to get some work done. What you'll see in the spring, however, isn't whole-house types of projects. You will see a lot of exterior work including roofing, foundations, patios, pools, and landscaping. Yet, most of this work can be done through the summer and fall months when you might get a better deal on outdoor products as stores to begin to clear the shelves for the winter months. You might also find more Pros that are able to give you competitive pricing.

Summer

When it comes to home improvement, things generally slow down dramatically in the summer months. Families are traveling on vacation or are entertaining houseguests, so they can't be bothered with major renovation projects in the middle of all that. In fact, in some areas of Canada, all construction grinds to a halt for July, just because there isn't enough work for Pros to want to remain available. This makes summer an excellent time to get a lot of work done on the interior of your home. Pros will enjoy being able to work indoors out of the hot sun. Plus, you'll get a jump on the competition, as people want to start getting their homes ready for winter. If you have a renovation project during summer, you may also consider having your HVAC heating unit system serviced, as many companies offer a discount during the summer months. Taking advantage of this won't just save you money, it will help you avoid emergency calls once winter begins.

Fall

Did you know that in the fall, Home Depot hires as many as 80,000 seasonal part-time workers? This is because fall is one of the busiest times of year for home improvements, driven by the holiday juggernaut that takes over once school is back in session. People who are hosting family or friends for the holidays start thinking about finally getting that kitchen, bathroom, guest room, or front entryway renovation done before they arrive. A lot of interior work gets done in the fall, but often the weather is still nice enough to get some of that siding, roofing, and foundation work is done when the weather is a little cooler, and you can get a discount from material suppliers and Pros.

Winter

Winter is a great time to start any type of interior project, as well, if you're able to put it off from the fall. In general, the first half of the winter can be a slow time of year for home improvements, with most people focusing on the holidays and paying off their holiday bills. As soon as January rolls around, it picks back up with people trying to make good on their New Year's resolutions. However, If you can plan ahead, this is the best time to purchase materials like tile, wood flooring, cabinetry, and stone. Why? Because many of supply warehouses hold big sales offering closeout pricing during January and February to help move product. You're likely to find great deals on these products as suppliers try to clear out inventory before the spring. By planning ahead, you could save a lot of money just by shifting some of your interior home improvements to winter, rather than taking them on in the fall. Think of it as planning ahead for the next holiday season a year early, rather than racing against the clock to fit it in right before the holidays are upon you.

Do Your Homework

While you'll be hiring a Pro to help you through a lot of the project, that doesn't relieve you of the responsibility of knowing what is going to happen to your home, or what you'll put in there. So, before you begin, take the time to do a little research into what's available, what you want, and what you think will work. Visit some showrooms, look through style mags, and try to narrow down what you want from this project. You can get as creative or involved as you like at this stage, just keep in mind that your Pro will likely have advice and input, so keep an open mind.

Set A Budget

Part of your research should tell you what the going rate is for home improvements in your area. Set at least a loose budget for your project; you can fine tune it after you speak to your Pro and they give you more specifics. There are a few ways to get a high-level ballpark number. Below are a few options ordered from the easiest to more involved:

- Online resources, such as <u>HomeAdvisor Cost Guide</u> or <u>HomeStratosphere</u> provide a cost range by project type
- Reach out to neighbors who recently completed a project like yours
- Have a Pro walk through your project and provide a high-level bid

Big Home Improvement Budget < Comp

For sizable home improvement project, such as major remodel or addition projects, it's a good idea to do a quick check against your real estate comp to ensure that your home improvement budget less than the home price around your area.

A quick side note, comp is short for the word "comparison," in this case, it's a comparison of your home and those located nearby or those that are similar in age, structure, and environment. At the time of a sale, comps are done to make sure that the home's value is within other similar homes. Your bank, insurance agent or realtor will look at your home's square footage, size, architectural style, general condition, unique attributes that it may have, and its location and try to find another home with similar characteristics. Once they locate that similar home, they find out how much that home last sold for and what its current value is. Ideally, your home will be selling for about the same amount, with fluctuations included for inflation, the general real estate market, and small details that your home may include that may affect its price.

Why Comps Are Done During Home Improvements

When you purchased your home, you probably heard your bank or your realtor talking about comps and how they may affect your mortgage, the house's sale price, or your homeowner's insurance. Comps are an essential part of any home buying process, but it's also crucial to have proper comps done before you begin a major renovation or remodel. Remember, any type of home improvement that you make on your home increases your home's value. This may sound like a good thing, and it usually is, but occasionally, this can backfire. For example, Jim lives in a 1940s ranch that is currently in keeping with the other ranch style homes in his neighborhood. He has never been fond of the ranch look, however, so he remodels, putting in luxury upgrades that include a renovated entryway, front "tower" to make the home more closely resemble a Colonial, and spacious kitchen and bathroom additions. Jim also puts an addition on the back of the home, changing the footprint and increasing the square footage. The home is beautiful, but in a few years when Jim goes to sell it, he finds that he can't — no one wants to pay what the home is now worth. Why? Because Jim's home is no longer in keeping with the rest of the ranches in the neighborhood. So its value is now artificially inflated. Jim has to make a choice: sell the house for what the neighboring houses sell for, taking a loss on his home improvement investments, or take the house off the market and continue to stay there in the hopes that other homes in the neighborhood will also undertake similar renovations.

If Jim had done his comps, he would have found out how much the most expensive ranch in his neighborhood was worth. He would have also seen what the average value was, and he could have scaled back his renovations to keep the house in line with these. This doesn't mean Jim should have forgone his renovations or skipped the addition, but he may have chosen different materials or decoded not to increase the square footage quite as much.

Doing your comps before a home renovation gives you the information you need to make better choices regarding your home and the investment you're making in it. Don't be a Jim.

Prepare for Contingency Budget

In a perfect world, your home improvement project would go off without a single hitch. You wouldn't have any delays, your Pro wouldn't find structural issues that needed to be corrected, and all of your materials would arrive right on time, without any damages. Too bad you live in the real-world, which is anything but perfect.

Unfortunately, these scenarios happen all too often to unsuspecting homeowners. You enter your project optimistically, thinking it will go accordingly to plan, only to have to stop, put things on hold, or try to come up with extra money to fix unforeseen problems, due to issues you never knew could occur. It's tempting to try to blame these things on your Pro, the last homeowner, or the materials supplier, but a lot of issues could be dealt with quickly if you have a contingency fund.

What Is a Contingency Fund?

A contingency fund allows you to have a little bit of peace of mind as you enter a large home improvement project. This is a portion of your budget that is earmarked just for potential problems or issues that may pop up once the project is underway. This money is set aside so that you can handle any issues as they occur and you don't have to stop or delay your project.

Unlike the rest of the money you set aside for your home improvements, a contingency fund is usually held in escrow if it's needed. In many cases, when you get a loan for your home improvements, you can stipulate that a portion is held in escrow as your contingency fund, which is released on an as-needed basis.

You should estimate that for a larger project, your contingency fund should be roughly 20% of what the total project should cost. For smaller projects, you should set aside approximately 10% extra to cover any issues.

Why Should You Have a Contingency Fund?

It's tough enough coming up with the funds necessary for your home improvement, so why should you try to come up with 10 to 20% extra? Because problems arise every day that you just couldn't have seen coming.

For example, say you're having an addition put onto your home, and when your Pro tear out of the area he'll be building onto, he discovers something like dry rot. Because this could compromise the structural integrity of your home, it needs to be addressed, and this extra work and materials need to be paid for.

Without a contingency fund, you could be looking at choices like these:

- Fix the dry rot, but scrap the rest of your project due to lack of funds
- Continue with your project while fixing the issue, but scale back on the quality of your materials and the scale of the project to make sure you can still fit it into your budget
- Stop the project temporarily while you try to get a second loan or otherwise come up with the extra money

With a contingency fund, your project could proceed as scheduled and the dry rot would be fixed at the same time. No extra delays, no scrambling, and no scaling back on the rest of the project. Most banks and other lenders are aware of the need for contingency funds, and will usually factor them into the total loan. If the funds are held in escrow, they can quickly return right to the bank if they aren't needed, reducing your total loan in the end.

Better Safe Than Sorry

Having a contingency fund is like having insurance. You hope you never need it but are very thankful for it if you ever do. Make sure you have one set aside for your project to ensure that everything goes off without a hitch. If you can't use part of your home during the renovation, like the kitchen or bathroom, or if you will need to move out, make sure you factor these costs in now, so you aren't taken unaware later. You can also think of it as a safety net; you might end up not needing it, but you'll be glad it's there — especially when you're up there on that highwire!

"Success depends upon previous preparation, and without such preparation there is sure to be failure."
- Confucius, Philosopher

Insider Tips

When you achieve mastery over your own mind, you can tackle your greatest challenges with calm, clarity, creativity, and laser-focused action. When you take command of your mind, you can activate its vastly unused powers to reach your potential. You'll need to recognize negative thinking, weaken those thoughts, and strengthen your mind with positive thought.

MIND TRAINING WORKSHEET

Negative Thinking	Change Mindset	Strengthen Your Mind
Example *I'm not good at reading* *this contract. I will* *totally get screwed.*	*It's okay. Take a long* *deep breath. I just* *haven't learned the* *special terms yet.*	*I will ask my architect* *to explain the details for* *me. Then, I can have a* *productive discussion with* *my contractor.*

11 Get Inspired, Be a Creative Badass, Get Your Squad, and Roll

Inspiration for your home improvement project is everywhere; magazines, television shows, and social media sites like Pinterest and Instagram have changed the way that people view home improvements. Most of them are great; it's now easier than ever to get inspiration and ideas for things you can do to improve your own home. Unfortunately, there is a downside to this recent publicizing of home improvements as well — the unrealistic expectations that give to homeowners when it's time to start their own projects. On top of all that, there are countless choices to consider, numbers to crunch, and decisions to make -- and that's all before things really get started!

The reality is that there are so many moving parts once you start the journey. It's no wonder some people get stressed out just thinking about the whole process, and start second-guessing themselves. They start doubting themselves, asking questions like, "Did I hire the right pros?" and "Would my ROI be better if I switched to hardwood flooring instead?" and "Is my wall color too bold?" And on and on in a downward spiral until they find themselves in a full blown panic attack. Don't give in to the self-doubt. You're different -- you are a boss. You've got this.

(DISCLAIMER: This isn't going to be all doom and gloom; we'll get through this together and make sure you find the balance between getting inspired, getting real, and getting the right squad to help you. There's a method to my madness, so bear with me.)

We call this paralysis by analysis. If you allow yourself to fall into this trap, it can stop even the most simple renovation projects in their tracks as you second guess every detail and decision to the point that you can't even feel safe to move forward. I want you to get inspired, not overwhelmed.

Up to this point, you've been doing a lot of background work on yourself and your project. You've worked your way through the journey of self-discovery and probably made some new realizations about yourself along the way. Hopefully, you've also learned that you are creative and that when it comes to your home, it's your opinion that matters.

Well, it's finally time. You're ready to start the renovation process and turn your home into the castle you've always known that it could be. So, where do you begin? The answer can be a little complicated, just because you have so many options for how you can start. That said, there are steps that you can take to prepare yourself for what's to come.

Accepting the fact that you can be creative and take charge of the planning of your project is one thing — but actually taking steps to do it is something else entirely. For some people, merely acknowledging that you want to be a part of the creative process is enough; working with a designer will help you unlock your potential, provided you're upfront and honest with them about what it is you want to see in the home.

For others, though, sometimes you need a little more help to get going — and that's perfectly fine! Everyone creates and gets inspiration in different ways, and it's okay to need a little help to get to where you're going.

These tips are designed to help you get your creative juices flowing. And even if you aren't able to dream up a finished interior, you'll still come away with a better sense of the creative process, as well as what you want to see within your home.

Get Inspired

Inspiration can be found in-person, in print, on television, and online; you get to choose where you draw from. Visit designer showrooms or open houses to get ideas. Flip through some design magazines and flag pages for reference. Or, hop in the information superhighway known as the Internet and engage in some online image search. There are many excellent home improvement sites like Houzz, HGTV, and social media like Pinterest and Instagram dedicated just to chasing down all sorts of images. Whether you prefer analog or digital, here are some hot tips to connect you with the inspiration that awaits ...

Online Inspiration

When you search online, there are plenty of tricks to help you find the images you want to see. Like finding a book in a library, you want to provide the search engine or social sites as much specific information as you can, so that it will return relevant results, e.g., "Contemporary bathroom large window corner freestanding tub." Most people provide generic terms, such as "bathroom remodeling," they spend hours be browsing through page after page of generic images. I used to work at Yahoo! Search Marketing and year after year, I continue to be amazed at the search pattern. Naturally, with the groupthink approach, people replicate the generic bathroom re-model image when remodeling their bathroom. If you are going to spend the time and money to improve your home, then **you do you**.

Between running a company and taking care of my kids, I don't have a lot of time to waste, so I subscribe to the model "do it once, do it right." I imagine you're pretty busy too and want to get things done efficiently, so let me share other search tips:

- **Reverse Image Search Using Images**
  Have you ever come across a photo of a house or a room that you really like, and you want to see more of it? Or if you want to know the design style? When you save an image and then search it on Google Images (with the camera button), you'll be able to see similar images.

- **Related Website Search**
  To find other websites with similar content to a website you already know of, type 'related:' in front of the website address that you already know.
  Example Search: related:google.com

- **Exact Phrase Use Quotes**
  This one is a commonly known, simple trick: searching a phrase in quotes will show results with the same words in the same order as what's in the quotes. This is useful, especially if you're trying to find results containing a specific phrase.
  Example Search: "Philip Johnson Glass House"

- **Unknown Word Search Use An Asterisk**
  This lesser-known trick is helpful if you're trying to determine a style, but you don't know how the exact name. Search for a phrase in quotes with an asterisk replacing a word, and it will search ALL VARIATIONS of that phrase!
  Example Search: "Philip Johnson Glass House * style"

- **Eliminate Results Containing Certain Words Use The Minus Sign**
  If you want to eliminate results with certain words that you aren't interested in seeing, you can put a minus sign in front of the terms you want to exclude. Say you want to

search freestanding tub, but you don't want to see results for clawfoot tubs. It's easy — just put the minus sign in front of word "clawfoot."

Example Search: Freestanding tub-clawfoot

- **Search Specific Websites For Keywords**
  If you want to search for a particular thing on a specific website, you can use the "site:" function. Think of it as a Google search within that particular website. Let's say you want to see the freestanding tub in houzz.com, you'd enter this:
  Example Search: Freestanding tub site:houzz.com

- **Related Search**
  If you want to discover new websites with similar content to a website you already know of, use the "related:" function:
  Example Search: related:pinterest.com

Don't Be Afraid to Go Analog

While Pinterest and Instagram are great places to look for inspiration, it can be a little overwhelming for people who aren't entirely sure of what it is they want. There are millions of images!

So, why not go analog and take yourself to the library or a bookshop that has a large magazine section. Take a pile of home interior magazines and a cup of coffee and go find yourself a comfortable seat.

Magazines feature professional photos that are usually well staged, beautifully lit, and artfully cropped, which means they are designed to get you to focus on specific aspects or details. Look through the magazines and mark any images you like. This is a tactile exercise that can be both calming and invigorating. It doesn't matter WHY you like them. It doesn't matter if this isn't exactly what you want your home to look like — just mark the images you like the look of. (Hot Tip: grab a stack of Post-Its so you can flag the pages that resonate with you.)

Often, you may respond to certain details without even realizing it. For example, I had a client who brought me a stack of kitchen pictures that she declared had nothing in common. Once I browsed through them, I found that they all had metal accent tiles in the backsplash. Clearly, she liked this small detail, and once I pointed it out, she relaxed and started getting more involved in designing her kitchen around those accents.

So, start by gathering images of things that catch your eye. Don't worry about analyzing what they have in common that comes later. For now, just trust your instincts and go with your flow! Even if they seem to have no common detail, your designer may be able to help you pull them together. Or, you may discover something yourself that inspires you for the next phase as you enjoy a leisurely flip through the pages!

See It In 3D: Go Window Shopping

You may call a designer who will likely have a set number of show-rooms they want you to visit. Or just search online, e.g., "Modern bathroom fixture showroom in Los Angeles" to get a list of show-rooms to visit. This is a great way to see and touch the finishes to understand how it will occupy space. Pictures are one thing, but the actual tactile sensation really engages your senses, giving you more information to help you make your decisions. Make an appointment with a design consultant there to get extra attention from the staff. Then, take a look at what's on display. Bring photos for reference and don't be afraid to ask for samples of things you like. Again, you aren't trying to make sense of things yet — you're merely getting a feel for what's available and what appeals to you. Once your design professionals start to design, you can ask for a 3D renderings so you can visually confirm the design direction.

Bring Your Inspiration To Life

By this time, you should have collected numerous magazines, images, and samples, as well as some preliminary ideas and sketches from your designer. It's time to play and have some fun.

Grab a few large pieces of poster board and lay them out on a table or the floor. Now, start arranging those images and samples together on the boards. You're basically creating a vision board for your design inspirations. You can include paint color cards, tile samples, fabric swatches, or photos of whole rooms. Arrange and rearrange. Hold samples up against one another to compare. Look at them in a variety of lights including outdoors and the room you're renovating. This is a tactile exercise to activate your brain on different levels to see how you respond to your ideas.

This isn't about deciding on any specific designs; you're merely getting ideas and a feel for what's possible. When you feel like you're onto something, set that board aside to show your designer later as a reference. Not only will they appreciate how much thought you put into it, but they'll also be able to use it to pull together some finished designs to show you later as part of your collaboration.

Trust Yourself

At the beginning of this chapter, I referred to paralysis by analysis. Luckily, you are NOT going to fall into that trap, because you've put in the work and time to give careful consideration to everything associated with your renovation. It's so critical to trust yourself, but also to know when to enlist the building and design professionals to help. You've evaluated your needs, your target budget, set realistic goals for what you want to achieve, and you've done the research to help you make informed decisions about what will be best for your home.

Trust that you've laid the groundwork and that's going to pay off. Sure, it's still going to feel a little intimidating. (I'd be shocked if it didn't!) That's okay. Feel it, process it, and take a deep, cleansing breath. Now is not the time to fall into the Catch-22 of a doubt — it's time to feel confident about your choices and forge ahead to achieve your new and improved home!

Get Creative!

The most common protest that a lot of people make when encouraged to get involved in the design process is that they're not creative. Stop selling yourself short! You ARE creative. You have plenty of creativity to tap into, you just haven't had an opportunity like this to fully engage it! So, ditch any misgivings or reservations about your creativity — it's time to shine.

The first is that you don't need to be a "creative type" to understand or appreciate the creative process. You don't need to have a design degree or be a working artist to be creative. It's possible to take part in the process by expressing yourself and articulating your likes and dislikes; you don't have to sketch them out, you just have to be able to describe them to the Pros you're working with on your renovation.

This is an exciting collaboration, and you should approach it with an open and enthusiastic mind. Your job is to share your inspiration research with your Pros and to communicate with them as they try to bring it to life in their design concept for your project. You don't need to actually create, draw, or design anything; you should choose a design professional who will put all of those pieces together for you.

Your job is to think long and hard about what you want to see in your space. This can be something as simple as wanting to include subway tile because you like the lines it creates, or it can be as complex as mixing and matching cabinet styles and colors close to one another to create visual impact with functionality that works for you. That counts as creativity!

You're not ultimately responsible for the finished design, nor are you required to be. It's up to your design professional to take your ideas, your creative input, and your opinions, and incorporate them all into the finished design. Then they present it to you, and as the client, you get to offer feedback and approve it, or send them back to the drawing board if things aren't quite right. Don't worry, that's part of the process! The goal is to make sure you're happy with the final design concept so you can confidently move forward.

You need to feel confident in your ideas and opinions. You know your space better than anyone, and you're the one who is going to live in it. Don't be afraid to voice your opinions and don't worry about your Pro judging you for it. This is part of the collaboration process, and it's their job to try to give you what you want, as well as to ask you for clarification if they are having trouble understanding an opinion or seeing things from your perspective.

After seven years of architecture design training, I learned that in the end, as long as you're happy with the final design that's what matters most. Rest assured that your opinions are entirely valid — particularly when it comes to your own home — so just focus on what you like and what makes you happy.

Your Voice Matters

Even people who don't view themselves as creative are still able to look at and enjoy art. They can appreciate it and the work that went into it. And this observation and appreciation is an essential part of the creative process; it's the other end that connects the circle and fuels the creative process. You don't have to be able to create the same art to enjoy it. It's like hopping on a flight to a destination; you aren't required to understand the aerodynamic and technical workings involved to take the trip. That's the pilot's job, not yours. To put it even more simple terms: you don't need to know how the sausage is made to enjoy the pizza.

It's important to keep this in mind as you think through what it is you want for your home. Don't worry about the creative part yet; whether you take part in this role with your designer or not is yet to be determined. Right now, you are merely acknowledging the fact that your opinion matters, particularly when it comes to your own home.

When your home project is complete, you want to look around and be happy. You want to feel proud of your home, and at peace with the way, it looks and functions. And you can't do that if you don't let your designer know what those things are that you enjoy.

Once you accept that you can have opinions and ideas and that it's totally OK to have opinions and ideas that differ from your design Pros, you can begin unlocking your own creative process. Even if all that process entails is identifying those images and materials that make you happy. Sometimes, the simplest type of creation occurs when you acknowledge to yourself the things that you enjoy looking at. From here, it's possible to continue with the rest of the process.

Enjoy Yourself

The hardest part of any of this is letting yourself go and enjoying the process. Once you get started, though, you may find that you're hard pressed to leave without at least a few idea boards of your own.

So, even if you take only the barest of forays into this sector at this point, just remind yourself this: Yes, you can create.

#SquadGoals - Get The Right Squad And Roll

A home renovation is a significant undertaking and, of course, you want everything to go smoothly and according to plan. To get the look, style, and function you want out of your project, you need to choose the right Pros to handle the job. That's right, it's time to assemble your squad!

Often I get asked by homeowners, "Should I hire an architect, a designer, or a contractor first?" It depends on the scope of work for your project. Think about the extent of your project. What components are involved? Is it only interior or exterior or both? Will there be changes to the existing structure, e.g., roof, ceiling, walls, floor, or foundation? What is it going to take to get the job done? Here's the most critical question: Who do you need on your team to get the job done? If you're doing a full kitchen remodel, you don't want to hire a basic handyman for the job; you hire a qualified design Pro who specializes in that area. It's not rocket science. This is your home, and you're making a significant investment into it, so choose your Pros wisely.

This section will give you a better understanding of the different Pros, and what they do, so you can determine exactly what help you need for your project. Understanding what each Pro does is the essential first step, selecting with the Pros who are compatible to collaborate with you is equally important. So, take it to the next level by choosing Pros who are compatible with you and your personality type. Think of a person or a group of people who you have an excellent working relationship with and think about their personality traits. Then reverse engineering the compatibility match to identify their personality traits. Voilà! You got your match. (See, there's always a method to the madness! That's why I had you go through that back in Chapter 3 — you're welcome.) Going into this collaboration should be exciting and fun, especially if you've chosen Pros who are aligned with your style and vision, so take the time to compare them during the vetting process to choose the best matches.

"Knowing Me, Knowing You, It's Best I Can Do ..."
- ABBA

Architect

Architects design building. For projects such as new buildings, new facades, sizable additions, a new configuration of the existing space with significant structural changes, historical preservation, or efficient and sustainable design, you need an architect. From planning, concept, and design to construction documents, building permits, and construction administration, architects are the best people to help you.

They work for and report directly to you, they ensure your aesthetic considerations mesh with the structural requirements for the design, that space is both livable and attractive and to current the building safety code to obtain the necessary permits to start the construction. If your project requires significant changes to the facade or height of your home, they will also prepare the necessary drawings for the building review committee to obtain approval. Architects can coordinate with engineers, general contractors, or designers, and often, your architect can help you manage the project all the way to completion.

Interior Designer

For projects, they focus on interior space planning and achieving a final cohesive look, such as kitchen, bathroom, bedroom, living room, designers are great partners to collaborate with. Although they don't usually have the training or the required licenses to deal with sizable interior structural changes, they will have to partner with licensed architectural, engineering, or construction firms who will perform such work.

Do your research and look at their work samples. Meet with them and see how your personalities match. Your designer will work closely with you to help realize your dreams; think of them as a translator, taking the language of your ideas and inspirations and communicating it through the finished look and feel of your home.

Decorator

While a designer is going to plan the layout and flow of your interior space, a decorator is a person you hire for the cosmetic decoration of your home's interior. Your decorator will help you choose this finishing touches of your interior, such as paint colors, furnishings, fabrics, draperies, accent pillows, etc., — all the things that help enhance your space and add the finishing touch to bring it all together.

Engineer

Engineers work with architects during the design phase to ensure that your home is safe to live in. In fact, they might be the reason your architect tells you that you can't get rid of that pesky column or move that wall and to add additional structural beams — because it prevents your roof from collapsing. If your project requires specialized structural, or civil, engineering services, you won't need to worry about interviewing and selecting an engineer; it's likely that your architect or builder will hire the engineer since they work with them on a regular basis. Just don't be afraid to do your homework and research their credentials and previous work — this is YOUR squad.

Design-Build Firms

A design-build firm has in-house teams of architects, designers, engineers, and contractors, allowing you to you to hire one firm to handle all aspects of the job from start to finish. Because all your Pros are in the same office, you can, streamline the process, simplify communication, and minimize your stress. This option is like a one-stop shop for those who don't want to hire different individual Pros. You might prefer this option for the sake of simplicity. Or, if you already have contacts or recommendations for Pros, by all means, go forth and conquer. Again, this is YOUR squad!

Builder

A lot of people confuse architects and builders. Remember, an architect will design your home. A builder will handle the construction of your new home, including setting the foundation, framing, and roofing, as well as erecting the walls. Most builders don't handle mechanical work such as heating and cooling, electrical, or plumbing.

Although a few may have some experience, the vast majority of builders are not trained in design. They build. If your project does not depend heavily on design, or if time is a factor, a builder may help you get the project done quickly. If you're building a custom home from scratch, you should always work with an architect to design it, then let the builder carry out the plans.

General Contractor

A general contractor (GC) supervises the day-to-day work at the construction site and controls the short-term schedule, managing the team of subcontractors, helping with the permit process, and monitoring the progress. They often have a superintendent or project coordinator on your project to coordinate the operations, as well as all the subcontractors (electricians, plumbers, roofers, etc.), which is where their true value lies. Plus, they're required to be licensed, and there are many different types of licenses in specific disciplines, such as roofing, which means they can also handle smaller renovations that are mostly cosmetic and don't involve significant design changes.

Who Is In Your Squad?

So back to the earlier question: "Should I hire an architect, a designer, or a contractor first?" Well, you know the answer. (1) If you care about the aesthetic and want to make changes to the existing structure, then hire an architect or a design-build firm. (2) If you want to build a brand new home, then hire an architect and a builder. (3) If you want to only focus on the interior space use furniture, fixtures, and other accessories to create a desired look and function for spaces inside a building, then hire a designer. (4) If you already have city-approved plans, then hire a general contractor. That was easy!

Leave It To The Pros: Design First, Then Build

It's easy to see designs on HGTV, Pinterest, Instagram, or on sites like Houzz and see thousands of designs for each room in your home, and get inspired and even tempted to copy them for your own space. You're getting inspired and tapping into your creativity — good for you! But beware, because attempting to copy a design created by trained design professional for a different space can be problematic without design assistance of your own.

It usually starts out innocently enough. You're planning a kitchen renovation, so you schedule a consultation with a design Pro to get the ball rolling. They ask you what kinds of designs you're drawn to, what ideas you have in mind, and what your likes and dislikes are, which causes you to go exploring magazines and websites. Then, instead of returning to your design Pro with your findings, you go rogue and attempt to copy those designs by hiring a builder to tackle the job. You know, because it'll be way cheaper and quicker.

Here's the problem: the design you like wasn't conceived with your home in mind, so your floor plan, color scheme, architecture, and other variables practically guarantee that the design is going to turn out very different from your expectations — and not in a good way. Here's another problem to consider: builders will do what you tell them to do, not what's best for the job.

Remember, most of them aren't trained in design, so instead of pointing out what could be a potential issue, they're going to build according to the plan. So, later, when running into trouble because your home doesn't pass code because of space considerations, or you realize that your new kitchen isn't anything like what you expected … it'll be too late. If only you'd used a design Pro!

Design Pros are able to advise you on how to make your design truly fit your lifestyle, how to make the room function better for YOU. That's what they do. You're unique, as is your home. Your design Pro takes the ideas and inspiration you bring, and they find a way to bring it to life to suit your world. They can actually save you money by making recommendations that can positively affect your bottom line. That's way more complex than just taking a picture from a magazine and trying to copy and paste it. That design you're trying to recreate? It was conceived by a design Pro. Whether choosing an individual Pro or with a design-build firm, you won't regret having their expertise.

It's A Job Interview: Hire The Right Pro

Hiring the right Pros for your project requires proper research and vetting. You want to assemble the best squad you can, and that means putting in some time and effort on the front end to avoid disaster later. You can avoid big problems later by hiring Pros who won't bring any problems to your project.

The Vetting Process

Most people get at least three bids or estimates for the work, but picking the cheapest bid isn't always the smart move. In many cases, choosing the most inexpensive option would result in costing more and taking a long time to finish the project. That sounds like an oxymoron. "How can I hire the cheapest contractor and end up cost more?!" Well, often these low bidders present a really cheap estimate, which omits some cost, possibly due to their innocent misunderstanding of the scope, or because they're using the bait-and-switch tactic. You know, intentionally bid low to get the job, then making up the difference through Change Orders.

Here is how it works: homeowners hire them and feel good about making smart money decisions by not paying more for the project. Then, their house is torn apart, leaving the homeowners in a vulnerable position. Like clockwork, that's when their contractors would request for Change Order to extend project cost and time from the original estimate. Unfortunately, by that time, the homeowners don't have a lot of negotiating leverage because their house and sanity are being held hostage.

They have two choices: give in and agree to their contractor's request, or fire the contractor and start all over again. Both options will leave the homeowners angry, stressed, and frustrated. Many them would choose the first option, agree to the terms, and suffer in silence because they're embarrassed about making a bad decision.

This is why vetting your Pros is so essential. It will give you a thorough understanding of who they are, what skills and expertise they possess, and most importantly, how ethical their business practices are. That sounds daunting, but you're going to trust these people with your most valuable asset — your home. Let me walk you through the key criteria so that you'll know how to evaluate them properly. Be thorough, not sorry. By taking the time to vet your Pros, you'll avoid problems such as:

- Legal and health safety liability exposure from unlicensed workers
- Pros without the necessary experience to handle your job, or the materials involved — which effectively means that your home improvement project is now their job training
- Conflicts due to you and the Pro having different visions
- Pros who suddenly depart your project for a new job, leaving you high and dry and your project unfinished
- Tension, stress, and resentment between you and your Pro are clashing over even the most minor details, due to your divergent personality types and work styles

And the list could go on and on ... but not for you. You're smart enough to recognize the value in investing your time in properly vetting your Pros.

Getting Background Information

The vetting process for your Pros actually starts the minute they walk through your door. Pay attention and take mental notes. How do they greet you — with warmth and sincerity, or with a calm demeanor? What is their body language — open and collaborative, or closed off and hesitant? This can tell you a lot about how compatible you are.

Next, you should ask to see their credentials and licenses: professional, business, driver's, and workman. You can verify their professional license with your state license board. To figure out your state licensing board, you can type in the type of professionals, the word license board, and the name of your state in the search box, e.g., "Contractor State License Board California." You can either enter the company name, company owner's name or the license number they provided. Be sure their license is in the "Active" status, which means they are legit and they comply with the requirement to maintain their license in good standing. This tells you that the Pros are who they say they are, are above board, and that they've taken the time to obtain licenses in their areas of expertise. Plus, you can verify that they reside locally, which makes them less likely ditch out on you and gives you ways to contact them. Don't be afraid to ask the following questions:

- How long have they been in business at their current address?
- How long at their previous addresses?
- If they have a regular crew, how long have they worked with them?
- What screening processes do they have for their employees? Do they conduct background checks, verify licensing and certifications, etc.?

- How do they handle subcontractors, if they use them?
- How would previous clients describe working with them?
- Have they filed bankruptcy Chapter 7, 11 and/or 13 in the past? If so how many times?

You can verify a lot of this information just by checking with the state, your town hall, DMV record, and the Better Business Bureau, so don't delay — get started as quickly as possible.

Ask for References

It's a best practice to get at least three recent local references from clients who had similar projects to yours. You Pro should have no problem providing these and should be eager for you to hear directly from other people who've been through the journey you're about to embark upon. When you speak to the references, you should ask:

- How satisfied were they with the Pro and the work they did?
- Did they encounter any problems with the Pro during the project? If so, how were those problems resolved?
- Did the Pro leave the job site upon completion of the project?
- Would they hire this Pro again or recommend them to their network?

In addition to the previous clients, you'll also want to obtain references from:

- Suppliers - so you can ensure there are no liens against the Pro for unpaid supplies.
- Manufacturers – particularly if the Pro recommends or sells a particular product. This will allow you to ask if the Pro has completed any additional training, received recent certifications, or if they are qualified to extend a

manufacturer's warranty on the product they're installing. This can be crucial for siding, windows, doors, and roofs.

Portfolio, Please!

In addition to references, you should ask to see examples of their work that is comparable to the job you're considering them for. This gives you a chance to check out their style and their work so you can determine if they have the experience required and if they'd be a good fit. (Remember, your instincts can tell you a lot — trust your gut!)

Whether it's an analog, old-school portfolio, or a digital version you can review online, they should be eager to share their work with you. After all, that's how they get more work! Be sure to specifically discuss any specialty product or materials you want to be installed that may require specialized knowledge to install correctly. If they can't describe the installation process to you in detail, consider that a red flag. Thank them for their time and move onto the next candidate!

Check Their Reputation

Don't hesitate to do some cyber-sleuthing and look up your Pro on the Google, Yelp, Houzz, Angie's List, Better Business Bureau, and other online reviews. You can uncover reviews, how long they've been in business, and if they've had any complaints made against them. A simple complaint is not necessarily a serious enough red flag to take them out of the running; what you want to see is how they handled and resolved the complaint.

Mistakes happen, complications arise. How did your Pro respond to the situation and did they make it right for the client? If you see multiple unresolved complaints, this could indicate a severe problem. (Think about Yelp! Reviews. Are you going to eat at a place with a slew of poor reviews? Doubtful!)

Remember To Trust Your Gut

How did you feel after the meeting with your Pro? Were you energized and excited about collaborating with them, or did you not really feel the connection? Did they listen to your input and respond to your questions? Is this someone you can see yourself working with for the duration of your project? Trust your gut, it won't steer you wrong. It's your project, your home, and your squad!

Do The Legwork Now So It Won't Cost You An Arm And A Leg Later

Yes, it takes time and effort to properly screen your Pros, this investment is your best defense against hiring the wrong person for the job. Spending the time vetting your Pros before you hire them might save you more time, pain, and financial strain later. Screening your Pro is time-consuming and sometimes awkward, but it's your best defense against numerous issues caused by hiring the wrong person for the job. We understand that this process takes up valuable time that you'd rather spend on getting straight down to business.

Take Charge Of Your Home And Your Squad

You are establishing a partnership between you and your Pro. They're going to be working in your home and around you and your family. You've hired them because you're trusting them to use their talents to transform your space. It's a delicate balance in the beginning; they work for you, and you're just getting acquainted, so you can't expect to be new best friends right out of the gate. Give it a little time for you to get on the same page and establish a rapport.

As you begin, remember that your Pro is not a mind reader. Every renovation project is as unique as the home and the family, and they're going to want to hear your input and ideas to ensure they are able to incorporate them in the design. Sure, they've got their own ideas, but they need to know your thoughts so they can ensure you're in alignment, so don't be threatened and don't clam up. You should tactfully assert yourself creatively, as well as strive to establish a working relationship which invites collaboration and effective communication.

Remember, you can set the tone for everything, so go in with the right attitude. You don't want to dread interacting with your Pros on a regular basis, nor do you want to be the client that makes them cringe every time they field an email or phone call, let alone when they're forced to interact with you in person!

You've already taken the time to vet them, you've seen their work samples, discussed your hopes and ideas, and you've decided that they are the right fit for the job at hand. You've added them to your squad. Now, you're in this together. You got inspired. You've proved you're a creative badass. Now, it's time to get your squad and roll!

#SquadGoals

"Imagination is more important than knowledge. Knowledge is limited. Imagination encircles the world."
- Albert Einstein, Physicist

Insider Tips

As a card-carrying Creative Badass and leader of your Squad, use this Creative Badass Game Plan to capture some essential information for each item. What do you want in each category? Start from the big picture to the details. Wait - this isn't a checklist ... it's a WISHLIST!! You've earned this, so go to town!

CREATIVE BADASS GAME PLAN

Category	Theme	How Does it Make You Feel?
Color Scheme	Primary: Accent:	
Style		
Fixtures		
Floor Material		
Finishes		

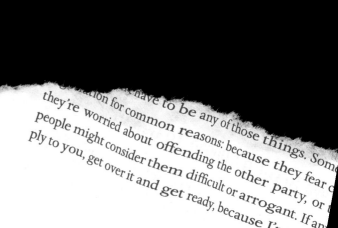

12 I'll Tell You What I Want
What I Really Really Want

The Spice Girls had the right idea: you should be able to communicate what you want and strive to attain it. Your Pro should be able to do the same. Even better, you should work together as a team! There's bound to be some back and forth, and once you both know what the other is after, you can start to work toward a win/win outcome. That's called negotiation, and you do it every day, whether you realize it or not.

You negotiate daily — with yourself, your friends, your coworkers, or your family, Everything from what you'll wear to work, to what to order for lunch, to what TV shows to watch. Those are simple negotiations, but what happens when things get more serious and complicate? We all know that a renovation project has many moving parts and factors, so don't be surprised if you and your Pro find yourselves on opposite sides of at least one issue at some point — and you're going to have to negotiate. Don't freakout, it happens to us all.

Negotiation is often viewed as scary, adversarial, or unpleasant — but it doesn't have to be any of those things. Some people dread negotiation for common reasons: because they fear confrontation, they're worried about offending the other party, or they're afraid people might consider them difficult or arrogant. If any of these apply to you, get over it and get ready, because I'm going to help you.

Here's a fun fact: it's not about making demands and getting what you want by any means necessary; it's about relationships and communication. It should involve both parties working together to gain a better understanding of the situation, discussing available options, and making compromises to reach a solution that works for both. Remember, you're in control, and it's all in the approach you take.

You actually have more experience with negotiation that you might realize. You've been negotiating with your parents your entire life, from the first few years of your life, using nonverbal communication, through your childhood and teen years. You and your parents negotiated bedtimes, when you would clean your room, and what your allowance would be. As you grew into an adult, you probably negotiated about curfews, cars, and college. See? You're already an experienced negotiator.

Whether it's regarding a budget issue, a necessary adjustment to your preferred design or a course correction if the project has gone astray, you can navigate the discussion, so both you and your Pro can get what each of you wants — with some. Get ready for a little negotiation boot camp …

"Everything is negotiable. Whether or not the negotiation is easy is another thing."
- Carrie Fisher, Actor

You Don't Have To Burn A Bridge To Get What You Want

A successful negotiation isn't one where only you get your way; it's when both sides feeling as though they got what they were after, or at least close to it. To achieve that outcome, you'll need to know what the most important thing is, both for you and for your Pro. Once you understand what matters most to each side, you'll be better equipped to discuss it productively. (This is another time when your Pro's personality style matters — and so does yours. Feel free to go back to Chapter 3 for a refresher.)

For example, let's say you want to add some decorative moldings to your dining room, but your Prois trying to tell you that he has a better idea for the job that will be less time-consuming and cost less. You're a big picture thinker, and you intuitively feel the molding will enhance the space when you're sitting down. Your Pro is more sensory and visually inclined and, after listening to his idea, you're still convinced that you want the moldings.

Now you need to negotiate this with her/him in a way that makes him feel considered and not dismissed; it's a civil discussion. You can even articulate your vision by showing him some pictures or drawings of how the moldings enhance the space to help him understand your position. It's not about winning the argument, or being right; it's about being objective and focus on your goal, which is getting those moldings up! Don't lose track of what's important and keep your eye on the prize!

Understanding Is Key

To prevent negotiations from breaking down before it even begins, it's crucial that you go in with an understanding of the issues from all perspectives. If both parties are just pushing their agendas, it's not going to be pretty. By demonstrating that you understand their position and priorities, you'll earn some brownie points, as well as the respect of your Pro.

After they present their side, you should try to restate what they're proposing so you can demonstrate you've been listening and to ensure you understand their concerns. "Let me make sure I've got this correct, and I know where you're coming from …" is an excellent way to start off the exchange. They'll respond in kind, and with both sides seeking to understand and not just trying to get their way, it sets a collaborative tone for the conversation, making your life much easier.

Everyone feels acknowledged, everyone feels heard, and everyone feels like they got a win. Cheers to that!

It's All about The Give And Take

The name of the game is collaboration, not confrontation. It's a series of quid pro quo exchanges between you and your Pro, as you work together to work toward what's most important to you. In the negotiation, you should always be ready and willing to concede something meaningful, but that doesn't jeopardize your end goal; your Pro will see you as willing to work with them, which will make them more likely to concede something when you need it.

For example, if your Pro is feeling a time crunch and there is a non-critical part of the project that could be pushed back, you could concede and allow them to finish that portion later. This doesn't affect the timeline of your project, but it gives them some breathing room. They'll appreciate your willingness to be flexible, and they'll remember it the next time you ask for something. It's about the give and take. Just don't forget that — like communication — it goes both ways.

Do It In Person

Think of some difficult conversations you've had in your life. Were they done in person? Over the phone? Via email or text? How did you feel about it after they were over? Anytime you need to have a difficult conversation, you should always do it in person. Factors such as body language, eye contact, and the surrounding environment can affect the interaction and help it be more productive.

If it's a conversation you're dreading having, you need to push past that fear and put your grown-up pants on. Having a tough talk face to face will earn you respect, plus it will remind you that you're both human, you're both ultimately working toward a common goal. These conversations never end up being as bad as you've built them up to be in your mind — remember that. Don't let your anxiety get the better of you; take a deep breath, take control, and take your time.

Choose a location that will be free of distraction where you can converse comfortably. Have a pen and paper handy to jot down notes and quick thoughts. Be mindful of your body language — make sure it's open and engaging, not closed off and stiff — it speaks as much as the words coming out of your mouth. Speak calmly and clearly, don't get emotional or aggressive. Be professional, direct, and remember to listen as much as you talk (if not more). Also, don't hesitate to bring any materials or documentation you might need to reference. If you need to calculate costs, your smartphone has a calculator on it.

Be Fair, But Firm

In life, you should always strive to be fair, but firm. As you work toward getting your goals met, it's critical to remember that your Pro has goals they want to achieve, too. You're taking the proactive approach, seeking to understand where they're coming from, and you're in control.

Be realistic and fair when communicating expectations, especially when dealing with timelines. It's okay to want your project done as quickly as possible, but it's not fair to ask your Pro to do anything that would put them in a compromising situation, just to get your project done. Nor is it fair to ask them to do anything that would jeopardize their integrity. In addition to the goals they want to meet, they have a crew to pay, materials to buy, and insurance to maintain so they can continue to grow their business.

Inevitably, there's bound to be some back and forth, some give and take on both sides. You'll give up a few minor things to ensure you get the big thing you want; that's just smart negotiating. When it comes to the major issues you consider non-negotiable, don't be afraid to stand firm. Explain your position. Explore other options that might work without you giving up what's most important. You can be firm without being rude, unprofessional, or aggressive. Stay strong and just explain that this is key to the design you envision, then ask what workarounds or options they might recommend. This puts the ball back in their court and shows that you're trying to work with them, not against them while asserting that you're standing firm.

It's Not Just What You Say — It's HOW You Say It

What you say matters, but HOW you say it is even more critical. In addition to using appropriate body language and demeanor, be aware of how you're saying things. I'm not just talking about making sure your tone isn't too pointed or aggressive; I'm suggesting that you subtly take control and guide the conversation. It's easier than you might think.

If your Pro is getting a little heated, then you can take things down a few notches merely by speaking in a calmer, quieter tone. This will trigger a subconscious reaction from them, causing them to adjust their tone and behavior to match yours. By using phrases that suggest collaboration instead of conflict, you'll take control of the conversation without them even realizing it. A simple question like, "What can we do to turn this around?" can change the entire situation — especially if you say it calmly, with warmth and sincerity. It forces everyone to stop and think for a minute, preventing unnecessary escalation. How you speak to others is as crucial as what you have to say, so stay calm, be cool, and be in control.

Listen, Listen, And Listen More

Most of the time, we're so busy talking and making sure people hear what we have to say, that we forget to listen. We'll sit across the table from them, watching their lips move, just waiting for the chance to jump in and say what we want to say. We're aware that they're speaking because we can hear that there is sound coming out of their mouth ... but that doesn't mean we're *listening*.

Smart negotiators are like good detectives: they ask probing questions, then they stop talking and start listening. If you're not listening actively and paying attention to what the other person is saying because you're too busy planning what you're going to say next, then you need to knock it off. Focus up and *listen* to the other person, so that when it's your turn to speak, what you have to say is actually applicable to the conversation. Otherwise, you risk looking foolish and impatient, which isn't the look you're going for.

Try using the 80/20 Rule: listen 80% of the time, and talk only 20% of the time. You'll be amazed how much you'll learn just by listening. Most conflicts or misunderstandings are a result of someone not listening. Pay attention, shut your mouth, and open your ears and you'll see how effective the 80/20 Rule is!

7 Ways to Say No (And Make it Feel Like YES)

"No" is the most powerful word in negotiation. Successful negotiators know when — and how — to say no. Saying "no" is not a personal rejection, it's simply stating that something doesn't work for you. You need to be comfortable and confident to disagree, rather than give in to something that isn't aligned with your ask. Prepare properly, know your options, be flexible, and be realistic. Here are 7 ways to say "no" without having it feel like a slap in the face to the person on the receiving end.

1. **No**: "I'd love to upgrade, but I'm going to have to decline due to budget constraints."
2. **No with Appreciation:** "I think your idea is fabulous and I appreciate your time, but I'm not able to commit right now."
3. **No with Values:** "If I approve this upgrade now, that would mean not being able to honor my commitment to take my family for a vacation before my kids head off to college."
4. **No with Help:** "I love that you thought of me, but I'm unable to, due to the timing. A friend of mine is thinking about doing the same type of upgrade, though — I would be happy to share your contact info with my friend."
5. **No and Yes:** "I'd love to upgrade, but I'm not ready right now — this month is too crazy. Can you ask me again next month?"
6. **No with Specific Yes:** "I'd love to talk to about your up-grade idea, but I'm on a deadline until Friday. Can we meet on Monday?"
7. **No When You Don't Know:** "That sounds interesting, I need to sleep on that for a bit." or "I need to check with my family."

With these 7 ways to say no, you need to tell the truth and stop talking once you said no. Be firm, be polite, and don't get pressured into saying "yes" to something you're not really ready to do.

"Price is what you pay, value is what you get."
- Warren Buffett, Business Magnate

Insider Tips

It's rational and imperative to do what all first-class negotiators do:

1. Research the market
2. Price out the materials, goods, and services accordingly
3. Begin to recognize the opportunity to negotiate $$$ for time and services
4. Practice asking what you want based on the value, rather than what we need to make ends meet

It's important to understand that getting the market value is not about just covering the expenses. For example, during the high season, the Pros are overwhelmed with requests or other external factors that Pros have little control over, such as an increase in the cost of materials due to the tariffs or shortage of supply. Be prepared and be informed. Do a bit of research to determine your values and priorities on both sides, so you reach the optimal agreement. Give it a go and practice making this list now so that when it's go time, you'll be ready to rock.

WANNABE WORKSHEET

What I Really Really Want?	What They Really Really Want?	Middle Ground

13 Decide. Commit. Succeed.

During my time at Beachbody, I learned this simple yet powerful concept of their tagline: "Decide. Commit. Succeed." It's one thing to see those words on a plaque or a poster, but it's even more powerful when you put those words into action.

You DECIDE to take on a renovation project. You've put in the legwork done all your research, selected your Pros, and settled on a design concept. It's time to pull the trigger finally. This is where the rubber meets the road, and things start happening.

Resist the temptation to visit just one more showroom, open one more magazine, or take one more scroll through Pinterest. Don't second guess yourself, don't doubt yourself. It's time to commit to the project. Stop lollygagging, stop stalling, stop making excuses why you should wait. COMMIT. Let's go.

Once you set the wheels in motion, keep reminding yourself of you WHY; this will help alleviate the inevitable frustration and stress that come from having your home space temporarily invaded and interrupted. Keep your eyes on the prize and your mind on you WHY, and you will SUCCEED. Three words, one simple mantra.

Trust Yourself, Trust The Process

Trust yourself. You've researched and approved the design concept, you've vetted and selected skilled Pros. It might seem overwhelming at times, but you need to remember that you're not in this alone. Your Pros understand the process flow, how things work, and the timing of decisions. This is what they do, so trust in their expertise and let them guide you through the process. Once you establish that trust, you'll be surprised how quickly and smoothly the process will move.

For example, in a kitchen remodel, once you choose a countertop and cabinet style, things like flooring, appliances, and backsplash will follow very quickly. Why? Because you've got a style, layout, and color palette in place, and those help dictate what remaining choices, making your life easier! The first few decisions you make might seem tough, but once you get into the groove and things start flowing, and you get into the groove. Trusting your Pros, the process, and yourself will make it easier to enjoy the project, and enjoy the end result even more.

Embrace Your Commitment and Focus On Your Project Success

Here's something to keep repeating to yourself: "Home improvement projects are a marathon, not a sprint." Although home repair work is a sprint, and sometimes it may feel like a marathon.

You've been working your way up to this moment; you've have dreamed about it, brainstormed, researched, and saved up for it for months -- or even years. You've selected the Pros you want to work with, you've signed the initial contracts, and it's about to get REAL. Now, you're at the starting line, waiting for that gun to go off to begin your renovation marathon officially.

Then you make one more pass on Pinterest, or you go to one

more showroom looking for inspiration, and you see something that you want to incorporate, or maybe it's something you like even better than what you've selected. Stop, breathe, and then breathe again. Don't get cold feet. Don't freak-out. Don't second-guess your choices. Remember a few chapters back when we talked about trusting yourself? Well, here's why ...

The Perils of Pulling Out: It'll Cost You!

Once your project begins, things begin to move quickly. Your Pro and their crew are working, preparing drawings, plans, and preparing your contract. Measurements have been taken, and materials have likely been ordered. The ball is in motion; and the train has left the station. At this point, any changes you make to the plan will result in project delays, and will likely mean you will accrue additional costs.

When you change things in the middle of the project, you'll see the effects quickly. In addition to the extra money your changes will cost you, you'll also have more stress, time, and aggravation. Both you and your Pro have invested time and money into the project, so each change has a ripple effect, impacting multiple people in multiple ways. This can affect the outcome of your project. Are you willing to jeopardize that? (Spoiler alert: NO.)

Pace Yourself

Remember, this is a marathon, not a sprint. You've put a tremendous amount of time and effort into your project (not to mention money!), so now is not the time to lose faith. Stick with your decisions, be confident in the choices you've made, and don't get distracted. When you think about pulling out, it's time to pull out your WHY. It's time to boss up and stay the course. Be smart and strong and pace yourself — your marathon is just beginning. I'll be there at every mile marker along the way to cheer you on, give you water, and feed you orange slices. (Because it's a marathon, get it?)

"The most difficult thing is the decision to act, the rest is merely tenacity."
- Amelia Earhart, Aviator

"Today, charting your own course isn't just more necessary than ever before. It's also much easier — and much more fun."
- P!NK, Global Pop Star and Authentic Badass

Insider Tips

To experience the best quality during your home improvement journey, you need to stop comparing, stop worrying, and *Just Do It*. Making decisions intentionally to help you move toward those things that truly matter to you. This worksheet can help you to visualize the tasks you need to complete and help to increase productivity and focus.

1. Identify all of the ideas/tasks with target dates under the "TO DO" column
2. Track your progress for each task
3. Move the task from TO DO, DOING, and to DONE.

FOCUS UP

(TIP: only focus on one task/to do at a time)

TO DO	DOING	DONE

PART III

14

Be Clear and Get Real: Communicate Your WHY/FI

Here's Why you Need To Share Your WHY …

Okay, you're about to get this reno underway. You've done your homework, you've assembled your squad of Pros, and you're ready to make your design concept a reality. Here's an essential question: Have you shared your **WHY** with your team?

You need to make sure your team understands the purpose of your project — not just the part about demolition and building new stuff — but why it matters to you, and what led you to start this home renovation. When they understand what it means to you, the client, it helps to personalize the project for them; it means that you're inviting them — and their talents — to be a part of it and to share your vision. In turn, they'll be more likely to produce amazing results.

While I was a graduate fellow for Professor Vincent Scully at Yale, I remembered he told a powerful old story about three bricklayers for the St. Paul's Cathedral in London. When the architect Sir Christopher Wren was inspecting the progress of the construction, he asked three bricklayers, "What are you doing?" The first man said that he was laying bricks. Then the second man answered that he was putting up a wall. Lastly, the third man responded that he was building a place of worship.

All three of bricklayers were all doing the same task, but how they themselves viewed their work couldn't be more different. The first man had a job; the second man had a career; the third man had a calling. Just to be clear, I'm not suggesting you should tell your Pro that your home is a place of worship. But the reason why I'm sharing this story is that there are three valuable lessons:

- Often when a group of people works together without a clear understanding of the goal can be challenging to get everyone on the same page; on the flip side of this coin is that many team members don't know how their efforts contribute to an overall goal, and this hurts morale and results in apathy
- Different team members can be involved in the same task but have very different ideas of its meaning and significance
- Share your WHY/FI –> understand HOW impacts others –> explain WHAT you want to achieve in a way that others can comprehend *(please feel free to reference Chapter 3 about different personality traits and preference to receive information)*

When you inspire your team to understand why they do what they do, you'll likely help elevate their sense of pride and appreciate their contribution.

One of my all-time favorite inspirational stories was about John F. Kennedy, who visited NASA and saw a janitor mopping up the floor. JFK asked him what his job was at NASA and the gentleman replied, "I'm helping send a man to the moon."

Sure, the man was a janitor, and his daily tasks were not in mission control or any of the astrophysics labs, but he knew what NASA was working toward and he felt a sense of ownership in the mission. Why? Because he was informed of what the mission was and he was included; he found dignity in his job, and felt a greater sense of purpose because he realized that he was contributing to the mission — even at his level. Profound stuff, huh?

Imagine how everyone working on your renovation might feel if they have an understanding of your **WHY**, and they feel valued for their contributions. Help your team understand the big picture your **WHY**, HOW, WHAT, and help create an environment of teamwork, so that everyone who is involved will be aligned with the shared expectations and move forward together towards the goal. Each small act adds up to something extraordinary.

Be Sure You Get It In Writing

Okay, you've chosen your Pros, selected your designs and materials, but as the homeowner, there's one more important step to take before you turn over the reins to your Pro — and it requires time and focus on your part: reading and understanding your contract.

Think of all the "terms and conditions" you probably just click "accept" on and proceed without reading through it all. I'm guilty of it, too ... but we're not just talking about updating your iTunes software — we're talking about the people who will be transforming your home and taking over your life, to some degree.

You need to read all contracts with your Pro thoroughly and make sure you understand what you agree to by signing them. Pay attention to what's in them, and what might be missing. There can be clauses that protect you, as well as clauses that protect your Pro. There might be clauses missing that should be included, which should cause serious issues down the road. If it's not clear, just ask your Pro to clarify or do some research before you sign anything.

In a perfect world, every Pro out there would have your best interests as their first concern, but we don't live in a perfect world. If you sign contracts without taking the time to read them, you could be signing a contract that specifies things that could make your life

difficult and affect how your project runs. Here are some key points
to consider when reviewing your contract(s):

- Ensure that the contract includes a specific start date! Do
  not promise the job to the Pro with an open-ended start
  date; that could mean that the Pro could put your project
  off indefinitely while making it impossible for you to hire
  someone else to do the job.
- Always ensure there's a clause releasing you from the contract if you are unsatisfied with the Pro's work.
- In some cases, you may also need to specify an end date by
  which all work will be completed, like finish the project before Thanksgiving, then include the Liquidated Damages
  clause in your contract. The Liquidated Damages are an
  amount of money that your Pros would need to agree to
  pay in case they breaches the contract by not finishing the
  work on time. It needs to be a specific type of breach of the
  contract, not any breach of any promise anywhere in the
  contract. Liquidated Damages are a pretty frequent feature
  in the construction contract.
- Include language specifying that change orders may be introduced during the work, changing the scope of the work
  so that the work can be done on time.
- Your contract should also very clearly state the terms of
  payment, as well as specify when each payment will be
  delivered. Otherwise, your Pro could ask for money up
  front, then never complete the end of the job.
- If there is insurance money involved, make sure the contract specifies that the Pro will be at meetings with the
  insurance adjuster to help you get your claim and that only
  half the money will be paid up front, with the final payment
  coming after approval from the insurance company and
  the satisfactory completion of the job.

- Check with your state to find out how much you should be paying up front; for example in California had set a limit to 10% or $1,000 or whichever is less for an initial deposit.

- If you agree to a payment schedule in the contract, be sure to also specify how much work needs to be completed at each stage, before that money can be released.

- Your contract should also include a clause releasing you from liens if your Pro doesn't pay suppliers or subcontractors after you pay him. Without this clause, you could find yourself in the position of having to pay for the work twice, or even be forced into selling your home to resolve the lien.

- Ensure that there's a clause that requires your Pros to clean up the job site when the work is done. Make sure that final payment is specified as coming after satisfactory completion of the job, which includes disposing of tear out and debris, and cleaning up the property. If you're having work done in sensitive areas, you can also specify in the contract that they protect these areas, such as hanging plastic sheeting to confine dust to one room, or covering landscaping with a tarp to ensure debris doesn't land in it.

- Make sure that your contract also details who will be working on the job if your Pro plans to use subcontractors or employees. You want to know who will be working on your home, and who is responsible for scheduling and arranging the schedules.

- Finally, always make sure your contract goes into detail what will be done on the job. Your contract should state step by step what will happen — now is the time to make sure that your Pro doesn't cut corners. If you and your Pro agreed on two coats of sealer on the floor, then two coats should be written into the contract. Otherwise, he might use one and call it a day.

Don't Lien On Me

You enter into an agreed upon contract with your Pro, you have the work done, you pay for the work, and you enjoy your new and improved home. That's how it's *supposed* to go. Unfortunately for some homeowners, a simple renovation project ends up with them facing a lien placed against their home. This can be a terrifying thing to happen to you, especially if you paid all your bills on time.

A lien can make it difficult for you to sell your property and, in a worst-case scenario, may even force you to sell your property in order to satisfy it. Protect yourself now by learning to know the two kinds of liens and under what circumstances they can be placed on your home:

Mechanic's Lien

This doesn't have anything to do with your car. It's a construction lien levied against your property for failure to pay for services rendered during a home improvement, renovation, or construction. It means that if a Pro completes the job in good faith and according to the contract, and you refuse to pay him, he can put a lien against your property to try to collect.

What?!?! Of course, you're going to pay your bills — especially if the work was completed to your satisfaction. Here's the catch: anyone who worked on your home is entitled to bring the lien if they weren't paid. For example, if your general contractor fails to pay a subcontractor, then the subcontractor can place a lien on your home, regardless of whether you paid the contractor or not. That means you could be on the hook for paying that amount twice or chasing down the General Contractor for payment.

Supplier's Lien

This is very similar to a mechanic's lien and is sometimes even called the same thing. In this case, the Pro may fail to pay his materials supplier, causing the supplier to place the lien on your home. Again, it does not matter if you already paid the Pro for the materials; if the supplier did not get paid, he has the right to take out a lien against your property.

What Can You Do

You can protect yourself from property liens, first by asking your Pro for a lien release clause, which can be written into the contract. The first thing you need to do is ask your Pro for a lien release, which releases you from any responsibility for the Pro not paying his bills. This is a great first line of defense, but some states may require a lien waiver, as well.

A lien waiver is something you can request your Pro bring you before each payment is made. It's a waiver from each person involved on the job saying they will not place a lien on your home. Some states will only allow a waiver once you have paid the Pro for each stage; other states will grant a waiver right at the beginning of the job. Check with your city or town hall to find out which applies to you, or look up your state's info.

Of course, you always have the option of eliminating the middleman and paying suppliers and subcontractors yourself, but this can turn into a logistical nightmare, depending on the size of your job. The choice is yours. Only you can decide if this extra step is worth it based on your Pro's reputation.

Finally, you also have the option of making a joint payment. For this purpose, you would specify that the payment you release is done jointly to the Pro and the subcontractor or supplier, increasing the chances that the third party will be paid.

Protect Yourself

An ounce of preparation goes a long way toward protection in the case of liens. This is why it's essential to research your Pro thoroughly, to ensure that they've always paid their bills in the past, helping to ensure the probability that they will continue to do so.

Take Control of Your Project

Your contract is not just a piece of paper you need to sign to get going, it's the legalese you need to sign to get going; it's the blueprint of how your project is going to go. Always take the time to read it from beginning to end, and don't be afraid to point out discrepancies or missing information to your Pro. Never sign anything you aren't sure of.

Manage Your Expectations

Assumptions are dangerous. Never assume anything going into home improvement, that way lies madness! Yes, you may think that this is going to be something quick, simple, or easy, but you can't possibly know that unless you are also a Pro who has seen countless similar scenarios.

Your Pro has likely seen it all, however, and will have answers and advice for you if you ask. Consider the following two scenarios:

Scenario 1:

Lisa is ready to remodel her kitchen. She's seen so many HGTV kitchen makeovers, she practically feels like a Pro herself. She has all kinds of ideas for how to make the space unique, and she's ready to go, expecting the whole thing to take about two or three weeks, tops.

Unfortunately for Lisa, all her ideas mean a lot more drawings by the designer, coupled with the need for custom cabinetry and specially ordered appliances, all of which bump out her total project timeline to about 16 weeks from the day she enters the showroom to the day her kitchen is done. (There's a reason it looks so easy on TV.)

Lisa is upset to discover that she'll be without a kitchen for a good part of this, as she expected the tear out and installation to only take two days at most. In the end, she goes over budget, loses sleep due to the stress of the project, and the project has been less than pleasurable ... all because she had unrealistic expectations. Poor Lisa.

Scenario 2:

Jennifer is also ready to remodel her kitchen. Unlike Lisa, she's done her research, knowing that things she sees on TV don't always show the whole story. Jennifer asks her designer lots of questions about things like lead time and how long a tear out will take. So, when the project ends up taking 8 weeks, she's prepared and has budgeted accordingly for things like take-out food while her kitchen is under construction. Her project finishes up when she expects it to, and she's thrilled with the results. Best of all, there are no surprises for Jennifer, because she did her research and asked her Pro every conceivable question.

The difference between these two projects lies in the expectations of the two homeowners. Lisa expects the magic of TV, while Jennifer expects a more realistic timeline. If Lisa had asked the necessary questions of her designer, things might have gone more smoothly. Don't be a Lisa, be a Jennifer.

Managing the Stress

At any point, when you find it challenging working with your Pro, ask yourself a few questions:

- Is the Pro attempting to communicate with you? If yes, this is a good sign that they are on your side.
- Are the issues coming up necessarily the Pro's fault? Sometimes they are, but often they may be beyond his control. Blaming him will not speed up the process of correcting them.

- Is the Pro working on fixing the issues? It may not seem as though the Pro is working quickly enough for you, but if they are working on the issue, you may need to step back and give them time. Some issues take weeks to fix, and you just need to exercise patience.

Are you feeling out of control? If so, remember this: You hired your Pro because he is an expert at what he does. You need to trust that he will do his job to the best of his ability; you need to step back from it and let them do their job. Jockeying for control will only create tension and could negatively impact the project. Instead, try asking your Pro for more communication so you can feel better informed about what's going on.

"Learning is not attained by chance, it must be sought for with ardor and diligence."
- Abigail Adams, American First Lady

Insider Tips

It's important to communicate your aspiration WHY/FI and help your Pros to understand your specific HOWs and WHATs, and the best to solidify your agreement is through a contract which you can document your expectations in your contract with them.

YOUR CONTRACT TERMS

Expectations	Your Ask
Target Start/Completion Date	
Project Schedule	
Payment Terms	
Lien Waiver	
Project Closeout	
Indirect (outdoor portable toilet)	
Cleanup	

15 What to Expect When You're Not Expecting
Navigate Through Common Mistakes

I'm just gonna give it to you straight: home improvements rarely go perfectly, without a hitch. In fact, they frequently have unexpected twists and turns, such as mold, asbestos, broken water pipes, and back ordered materials. My advice to you is to be realistic and expect some mishaps, that way, you'll be better able to think on your feet and stay on track. As mentioned in the previous chapter, when your team knows your WHY, there's a renewed sense of drive within the team, which drives you all to power through any complications.

Plan for Setbacks

Here's another Fun fact: we all dream. In these dreams, everything goes smoothly, runs according to schedule, and turns out exactly as expected. Dreams can be incredibly motivating, and they're good because they allow you to exercise your creativity and envision what you truly want. For example, when you're dreaming of your new home improvements, you can probably picture your new kitchen, the new colors, the new floors, new windows. Maybe you even envision the custom cabinetry, new surfaces, and appliances. Again, dreams are good.

But the thing about dreams is they tend not to be grounded in reality, and they often fail to include less fun dream subjects such as hidden mold, broken tile shipments, back ordered appliances, and burst pipes. These are just a sampling of the challenges that can be a very real part of even the most charmed, problem-free home improvement projects.

Remember the home improvement nightmare that I mentioned earlier in the Introduction section? Well, it all started with a leak ...

Of course, most of the unexpected major projects have the worst timing. I embarked on a bathroom renovation project to correct a water damage problem in my second-floor bathroom. Lucky for me, I was swamped with work. The water damage didn't care about my schedule, though. I had to get it fixed. I followed the same approach that I used for our previous projects, one that many homeowners follow; I got referrals from friends, family members, and neighbors. I searched online for reputable professionals, and I scanned through long lists of reviews. After what seemed to be extensive research, I hired this guy who was referred by my neighbors. I verified that the contractor was properly licensed and insured and I was off to a good start — or so I thought.

Before I signed the contract, I shared with him that I was trained in the field of architecture, and I'd some experience in building and renovating homes. He was younger than me and managed everything on paper, e.g., carbon copy paper contract, occasionally he use text and email as the secondary method of communication. When he did speak with me, he was condescending and talked down to me. In fact, when I shared with him about what I had in mind for the replacement of the ceiling, he told me, "It won't look good, and it's a stupid idea." Despite his attitude, I tried to maintain a positive interaction and work with him, despite it having been over a month since I'd sent him a picture that I'd seen with a similar scope. He didn't want to listen and gave me every reason why he wouldn't do what I suggested.

I was ready to roll up my sleeves and get ready to work. I even offered to purchase the material and do the millwork myself. (Yes, I spent numerous months in the woodshop as part of architecture school training. I've got skills.) He didn't want to budge. So, I communicated with him that if he were unwilling to do what I requested, I would subcontract out that work to someone else. He looked at me snarkily like I wouldn't know how to manage that on my own. After a frustrating month back and forth with his attitude, I found a carpenter who can do what I had requested and was ready to hire him. "You don't know what you're doing, and it'll look ugly," my contractor said, rolling his eyes. Then, I politely asked to issue a Change Order to reduce this ceiling work from the original contract. Considering he didn't have to do any of the ceiling work, he only deducted 30% instead of 100% of the original cost to do the work. As you may have figured out, I lost trust in him and just wanted him out of my house.

Shortly after the exchange, we were about two-thirds of the way through the project, and he invoiced me the final payment, including the ceiling work that he didn't do, along with remaining tasks that he hadn't yet completed. This was before the city's final inspection and before the punch-list was addressed. The one-month project ran over by three months. The whole experience caused stress and frustration for my entire family, not to mention the tension it created with our neighbors, who referred the contractor. Fortunately, I tracked his progress diligently and kept detailed documentation of everything. I withheld the final payment, asked him to complete the project, then informed him that I would release the final payment when the job was completed.

It's such a frustrating experience. When I shared my experience, some of my friends opened up with their own home improvement horror stories. It turned out they were too embarrassed to admit that they'd made a mistake and didn't want to shine a light on their mishaps, so they chose to suffer in silence. Invaluable lessons were learned; among them, how critical it is to find the right Pro who is compatible with you and willing to collaborate. I also learned that I needed to step up and negotiate more effectively. As much of a hassle as it was at the time, that nightmare has become a dream, because it set me on the path to share my experiences with you to make your life a little easier.

Get Over It - Mistake Happens

For example, if you ask your Pro about potential issues you may encounter, and he mentions mold, you'll be less shocked if you get a call notifying you that they discovered mold. Instead of being thrown for a loop and delaying your project, you'll be able to react quickly and decisively, calling in a remediation team to sort it out ASAP.

Remember, what you see on reality television is not reality; it's scripted and edited to tell a story that happens in "the real world." Let's say you or your Pro make a mistake. You might feel annoyed, embarrassed, or discouraged. You might even want to avoid that subject for the time being; that's a natural response. Newsflash: you guys are human! Do you really think you're the first one to make that mistake? Not bloody likely. Mistakes happen all the time; you aren't the first, and you won't be the last to make them -- especially in the realm of renovation projects.

Just resign yourself to the fact that mistakes — both small and large — will happen. Repeatedly. It's all part of this glorious thing called life! Don't let fear of making mistakes, or the embarrassment of mistakes you've made derail your project, or, even worse, keep you from getting started.

A mistake is an unintentional error. Nobody is going to judge you for making an honest mistake -- but they might judge you if you keep making the same mistake! Mistakes are learning opportunities that allow you to gain wisdom and apply it to future situations and choices so you can do better. This book might tip you off to some of the more common mistakes in the renovation process so you can avoid them -- or, at the very least, navigate them more easily if you encounter them.

The Power of Preparation

G.I. Joe was right — knowing IS half the battle! When you know there are going to be setbacks and challenges, you can mentally prepare yourself to handle them, enabling you to respond quickly without stumbling. That mental preparation can turn a potential catastrophe into a minor, momentary hiccup. When you take the time to map out what can go wrong, you will increase your chance to avoid potential nightmares.

Take airline pilots, for example; they log thousands of hours in training and simulations, planning for every conceivable problem scenario. They are mentally prepared for problems because they know it's not a matter of "if," it's a matter of "when" — and they need to be able to react quickly when something goes wrong because they're responsible for hundreds of lives every single day of their life.

A perfect example of the importance of mental preparation is Qantas Airlines Flight 32 in 2010. The aircraft used for this flight was an Airbus A380, the world's largest and most complex commercial jumbo double-decker jet, known as the "Titanic of the Sky" due to its size and capabilities. Minutes after takeoff, the aircraft's #2 engine exploded, just after ascending to 7,400 feet.

That was bad enough, but then the plane's incredibly advanced computer system failed, rendering the plane virtually un-flyable. The pilots could have panicked and made things even worse, but instead, they kept their cool and were able to complete a safe emergency landing, saving all 469 people onboard.

What should have been a deadly catastrophe was averted, and lives were saved, thanks to the mental preparation of the pilots;

because they were mentally prepared for the inevitable crisis situations, the pilots were able to think on their feet and walk away from the landing. (You can watch the documentary on YouTube for the full story.)

This mindset is commonly practiced in multiple industries and is often referred to as a "pre-mortem," in which a project team begins with the failure of the project, then they work backward to identify any potential contributing factors to the failure. What they are actually doing is reverse engineering a successful outcome by preparing for setbacks, identifying problems, and putting together an action plan for how to deal with them when they arise.

Common Scenarios

Many things that can go wrong in a home improvement project, and you need to resign yourself to the fact that some of them will be out of your control. Materials or fixtures arrive damaged. The vendor ships the wrong item, and then your contractor installs it anyway. You don't order the correct amount of material for space. These are all common mistakes, so don't lose heart. What you *can* control is how you deal with these mistakes when they do happen. Let's start with some of the most common problems, as well as how to avoid them …

Shoddy Work

You're paying good money, and when it comes to the work done on your home, you expect a certain level of quality. Shoddy work can happen anywhere, and while some people believe the old adage, "You get what you pay for!" That isn't always true. Paying more for a job isn't a guarantee that it's going to get done correctly.

How can you protect yourself from shoddy work? Properly vetting your Pros is the most critical step. Whether it's your painters, pavers, roofers, builders, or contractors, get and verify their references, examine their portfolio so you can see their previous work, verify the validity of their licenses, and research their standing with the Better Business Bureau to gather as much info as possible.

Work Left Undone

Imagine the frustration of discovering that the job you hired someone to do hasn't been completed — even though you've already paid for the work. While most states actually have laws designed to help protect you by limiting the amount you should pay your Pro before work begins, many unscrupulous workers will ask for half or even the full amount upfront. Receiving the money upfront gives them no incentive to finish the job, much less complete it to your satisfaction. Jobs involving an insurance payout or grant money from a natural disaster are two common scenarios where a so-called Pro gets the money in advance, starts a job, but never finishes it.

What you can do to protect yourself? Make sure your Pro is licensed and LOCAL. If you hire someone from out of state, it's easier for them to flee the scene of your job site, leaving you high and dry. You want someone local who has business ties and other customers and suppliers in the area that can vouch for them.

Ensure that your Pro is licensed because that means you can hold them accountable for the work being completed. For large jobs, you might want to negotiate a payment schedule, paying a certain percentage upon completion of each phase of the project. This is relatively common, and your Pro should be open to this. Regardless, you should never pay more than a small deposit, and you should never pay more than half the money up front. Depending on your location, you should research your state's building laws to determine how much you should expect to pay before the work begins.

Damage to Your Property

You're renovating your home to improve it, but sometimes the project can leave other areas of your home in worse condition than before work began. Property damage is one of the most common complaints, with thousands of cases pursued each year. Imagine a plumber damaging your tile, or a roofer inadvertently putting his foot through a skylight. It could be something as simple as workers not bothering to clean up after themselves, leaving your property a mess, which could also pose a safety risk, like nails, glass, or other debris behind.

How can you prevent this? Well, remember in the last chapter when I gave you that handy bullet list or items you should have specified in your contract? This is why. Having the detailed contract defining the scope of what want you and what your Pro is responsible such as cleanup and for leaving the rest of your property in the condition it was found in will help avoid future drama. If a wall needs to be opened to access pipes, or if secondary work is necessary, make sure your Pro discusses it with you first to ensure that you're aware before it happens. You can also make sure to double check with the references you call that your Pro has a record of cleaning up after the job so that you aren't left doing it.

If damage does occur, be sure to document everything with pictures as soon as you discover it. If your camera has a date feature, use this as well, so if you have to confront your Pro about the work later, you have proof that this is the way they left the job.

Disagreements

Remember, most home improvements can take weeks to months to complete, which means you'll be seeing a lot of your Pro. Ideally, you'll get along together and can iron out any problems quickly and easily, but if you and your Pro don't get along, you could find yourself caught in multiple, daily disagreements about how the work should be carried out. Remember; you're the homeowner and the one paying for the job. Your Pro should satisfy you and your expectations within reason. Otherwise, you could find yourself embroiled in a battle for your own home and the way it looks and functions. It just reinforces how critical it is for you to choose Pros who mesh well with your personality style.

Take Inventory

During any major project, you're going to start receiving shipments of materials, especially if you're going the DIY route, you're handling the ordering, or your Pro wants them shipped directly to your job site. You might be tempted to tuck the boxes out of sight until they are needed, but let's talk about why that could be a costly mistake. It's always best to open and inspect the contents of every box as it gets there to avoid complications like this:

Joan is having a bathroom remodeled, so she orders custom tile for the walls, and waits weeks for them to arrive. The boxes come, she puts them -- unopened -- into the bathroom for the installer, then she heads out of town for a week while the bathroom is being finished. (Can you see where this is going? Joan is not going to be happy at the end of this paragraph.) Joan returns, only to find that -- GASP! -- the wrong tile is on her walls, not the tile she ordered. To make matters worse, she can't return the tile and get the right ones, because to remove it from the walls would damage it. Joan now has two options; living with the wrong tile, or reordering, demolishing and installing at her expense. (We told you Joan would not be a happy camper.)

If she had just opened up the boxes and checked them upon arrival, this snafu could've been avoided. At the very least, she should've opened them up to check them before she left town and the installer was left to execute his part of the job. Get into the habit of always checking the boxes of everything as they arrive to make sure you get what you ordered. Don't assume your Pro will know if something is right or not; he likely has a lot of jobs and may not remember what you wanted. Don't be like Joan. Be proactive and check so if there has been a mistake, it can be corrected promptly — before it's too late.

The Clock Is Ticking

The same principle applies to check to ensure that none of the materials you've ordered are damaged on delivery. You don't want to let materials sit around unopened until your Pro is ready to install, only to open the boxes and discover that multiple tiles are cracked and will need to be replaced. This delays the installation, as well as your project overall, which will cost you more money. You'll want to verify the vendor's return and exchange policy and make a note of it, so you don't let the time window expire, which means you're out for the cost of the damaged tiles that can no longer be returned, as well as having to repurchase replacement tiles — and the added frustration of the inconvenience.

Over-Ordering

One of the most common mistakes is over-ordering materials, especially on small projects. Whether you're ordering your own material and merely having someone put it in, or you're tackling something DIY, you're going to need to measure and calculate how much material you need. Triple check — don't rush it; be thorough and accurate. Taking the time to get the calculations right will save you valuable time and prevent headaches down the road.

On the flip side, under-order is problematic, but it's not the end of the world, as you can generally get more of something unless you're purchasing a closeout or odd lot. Over-ordering, however, is very common. It's wise to factor in an extra 20% to cover breakage and future repairs. Beyond that, you may be wasting money, as the material may not be returnable after a certain time period.

Here's another example to illustrate that point:

Patrick was remodeling his entryway, and wanted a particular marble mosaic for inset in the middle, with matching marble around the perimeter. He roughly worked out that the room was 9 by 8 and figured out how much he wanted. He placed the order and then waited a few months before hiring someone to put it in. At this time, he discovered that he had nearly twice as much material as he really needed because he didn't account for the built-in benches in the room taking up space on either side or the fact that he needed less mosaic to fill in the center when the perimeter was brought in.

He found that because several months had passed, he couldn't return the marble, and he was forced to keep it, which meant the project cost thousands more than it should have. This could have been fixed if he had his Pro do the measurements for him. Don't be like Patrick.

When in doubt, lean on your Pro, and always have a professional double check all your figures before you bite off more than you can chew. This also goes for standard measurements. We know someone who ordered a toilet without realizing that they come in three sizes. He was upset to discover that his new toilet had a gap between the tank and the wall and that because the toilet had been installed, it could not be returned. A simple call to a plumber would have solved this issue much earlier.

Rushing and Last-Minute Orders

You've probably planned your project for months, if not years. Yet, when the time comes, you may find that your Pro can either work right away or not for another 6 months because he's fully booked. So, you find yourself rushing to make decisions. Unfortunately, this can lead to even more mistakes and errors.

One way to prevent this is to THINK STRATEGICALLY. Do your homework. Find out how much time things take to arrive once ordered so you can start to map out a timeline. Don't wait to schedule your Pro! Find out what their booking schedule is well in advance, as they have multiple clients and timelines to consider. You'll want to lock in the dates for your renovation on their calendar. Be prepared to adjust your plans according to their availability; although it might be frustrating, it won't kill you to delay your project until your Pro is free. Obviously, if there is a safety or health hazard such as asbestos or mold, that dictates immediate action and an increased sense of urgency.

Here's another cautionary tale:

Cindy wanted to host the holidays at her home, and her newly remodeled kitchen would enable to do it up Martha Stewart style. In September, she contacted a kitchen designer to get started, only to be horrified to learn that most projects take 6 to 8 weeks from time of tear out! Despite this roadblock, she thought she'd still be able to squeeze it in under the wire. Alas, she didn't count on lead times for the custom cabinets and special ordered appliances and flooring she wanted for her dream kitchen.

Faced with the choice of not having her kitchen for the holidays or needing to choose in-stock items, she foolishly decided to rush. Unfortunately, the in-stock selection was smaller than she wanted, making it hard to coordinate all the items together. It became a perfect storm of challenges; shipments kept getting delayed, work took longer than anticipated, and colors didn't match perfectly in the light of her kitchen once they arrived. While she did have a new kitchen in time for her guests, it wasn't the kitchen she'd dreamt about, plus her stress levels and costs were much higher.

Although not ideal, Cindy could have waited to start the re-model, once all the things she wanted had arrived. This would have afforded her time to perfect the space and create the custom kitchen of her dreams and hosted the next round, but her impatience and rash decisions resulted in her compromising her dream kitchen and settling for less than the ideal renovation. Now, each time Cindy cooks in her new-but-not-perfect kitchen, she probably has a tinge of regret to go along with whatever meal she is preparing. Hopefully, she learned a valuable lesson from experience. What's a lesson you can take away? Don't be like Cindy.

NOTE: Unless you have a health risk situation like a water leak, black mold, or some old linoleum just peeled up exposing asbestos fiber, you can always wait to have your project done right. It's worth getting it right the first time, without the added stress or expense.

Anticipate The Issues

What can you do? Make sure that you get along with your Pro by interviewing at least three candidates to see whose vision lines up best with yours. Or use our matching service that will not only vet your Pro but will match you on personality and vision as well so that you know that you're both in sync.

Remember, your Pro also needs to be in sync and in agreement with you; watch for subtle clues that he or she may not want the job to avoid conflicts later on. Your home improvement project is a collaboration between the two of you, so make sure you're both equally invested. Refer back to Chapter 12 to tips on negotiation. Protect Yourself and Your Property

Many common home improvement complaints can be solved by merely vetting your Pro and following through on things like contracts and doubling checking references. We know that these are time-consuming steps, so sign up today to let us do the work for you, and you can proceed with your home improvement project without cause for concern.

Acknowledge The Issue

Think back to when we discussed acknowledging your fears and how doing so will help you move forward with your project. The same thinking applies here. Setbacks are inevitable, and you're going to experience a few hiccups along the way -- that's the reality. Just accept that at the outset so that when it happens, it doesn't throw you for a loop; instead, you'll handle any setback like a true boss and keep the project moving.

Think about everything that has to happen during a project. The tear out, the ordering, the arrival of materials, the number of people that will work on it, the installation, the painting, the finishing. Frankly, it would be a freakin' miracle if it all went off without a single hitch. There are just too many different components in play here for things to go off entirely smoothly. We don't say this to bum you out or scare you; we are just trying to manage your expectations and help you succeed. Then, when you start planning for your project, you'll be anticipating setbacks, and you'll already be prepared to handle them without missing a beat.

And that it's not a question of if an issue arises, but when.

Dealing with the Issue

Don't forget that your attitude makes all the difference. Instead of seeing setbacks reasons why your project might fail, try looking at them as a problem that needs to be solved. You're in control of solving the problem. These setbacks are not insurmountable obstacles to your success; they're opportunities for you to employ your preparation and patience and to demonstrate you're in control.

Shifting Your Mindset

Imagine this scenario playing out two different ways:

Pauline begins a brand new renovation of her home, but when the contractor Jake starts to pull up the old, dirty carpeting, he discovers asbestos tiles underneath. And worse, the tiles are loose and potentially releasing fibers. Work comes to a halt as an abatement team is called in.

Scenario 1: Pauline is very upset, which is understandable, considering the expense and dangers involved. However, rather than attempting to stop and acknowledge and properly deal with her emotions, she lets them overwhelm her. She berates the Jake for not knowing the tiles were there in the first place and blames him for not being more careful taking up the carpet so that the tiles could have been encapsulated again more easily without the need for abatement. She becomes so focused on the setbacks -- the unexpected cost of living in a hotel while her home is cleaned, as well as the cost of the abatement services -- that she cancels a large part of the rest of the project, and is generally unhappy with the results. She will forever blame Jake for the fall of this project. When every time she thinks about the experience, she'll relive those emotions over and over again.

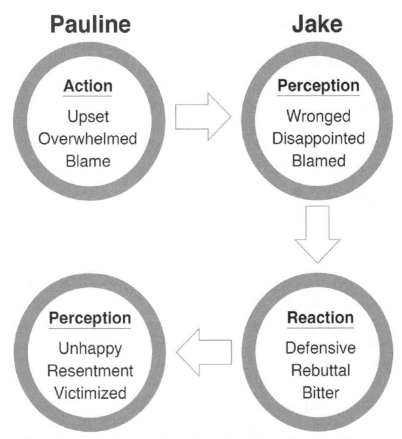

Fig. 2 Scenario 1: Action -> Perception -> Reaction -> Perception Diagram.

Scenario 2, Pauline is still upset, but she also acknowledges that things like this can happen in old homes. She allows herself a momentary freak-out, but then she remembers her contingency fund, which will cover the costs of the abatement and the hotel. She also realizes that when the renovation is complete, her home will safer and healthier than it was before it began, which allows her to breathe a huge sigh of relief. Further, she focuses on the fact that she got rid of both that old carpet AND some hazardous tiles at the same time, choosing to view it as an added bonus. Again, attitude is everything.

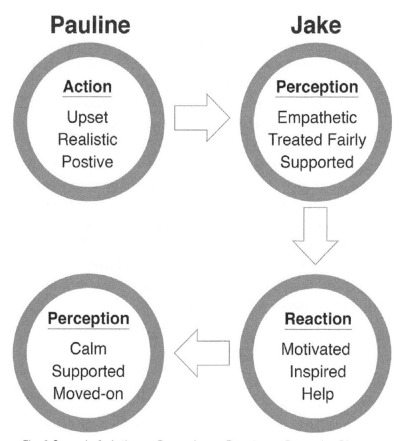

Fig. 3 Scenario 2: Action -> Perception -> Reaction -> Perception Diagram.

I know it's easier said than done, I'll give you that, but trust me it will be worth it. You know you're in control, you have choices - You can let that fear paralyze you, or you can shift your mindset. The fact that you have options to choose is the ultimate power. You can change the way you think about your fears, let your fear fuel your fight, and overcome those fears. So, which attitude are YOU gonna choose? *(Spoiler alert: It should be scenario #2.)*

Be Mindful Of Your Emotions

- Having a sense of control over your choices results in higher quality, increased productivity, and self-motivation.
- Communicating with a learning mindset leads to increased creativity, improved growth, and better collaboration skills.
- Praising your team for their hard work motivates them and encourages a greater sense of pride in their work.

Being in control of your emotion and behavior doesn't mean give up all spontaneity; instead, it means being mindful of what and how you're doing and redirecting yourself when you're heading in a wrong direction. If you can learn to manage those emotions and behavior and how you deal with situations, not only will it help with your own self-esteem, but you'll also build better relationships with others. Learn to take charge of a situation, master your emotions, and live the life you want to live.

Control an Immediate Situation

When you think someone may have wronged you, instead of reacting to the situation, the first thing is to focus on calming yourself at the moment. Often when people are upset, they start to lose control of their behavior. To master the situation and avoid those explosive reactions, you need to take a few minutes to calm down. There are a few exercises that you can to do to take back the control. You may want to practice them when you're by yourself now. That way, you'll know exactly what to do when you are in a critical moment.

- Take a deep breath and slowly exhale — counting slowly to seven as you inhale, counting slowly to seven as you hold, and counting slowly to seven as you exhale.
- Say aloud in your head that it's just a short-term situation.
- See your counterpart as a person with feelings and hopes.
- Don't get distracted by details.
- Don't lose sight of the big picture.
- Remind yourself to calm down.

When your mind is calm, collect your thoughts, form a plan to address the issue before speaking.

If you are still upset, walk away and come back when you are ready. It's possible you are reacting to miscommunication or misunderstanding. When your mind has calm down, you may want to talk it through with the person, listen to what they have to say to clear the confusion and get closure.

If after the talk you still have lingering negative feelings, then try these exercises to work through those emotions. Don't try to repress your feelings, because when you do, you won't control them. Instead, they'll control you. Write down your feelings. Reflect on what led you to that feeling.

If it's a triggered emotion, by means of this feeling always surface when a similar situation occurs, then you need to figure out what thing that you can do to avoid that trigger. You may also talk to someone to digger deeper to figure out the root cause.

Acknowledge those feelings, and name them

Like Elsa from Frozen let go of negative emotions. The beautiful part when you forgive those who have wronged you, you will develop empathy and compassion for those who have betrayed you. Forgiveness doesn't mean that you condone bad acts - it just means that you release the negative feelings associated with those acts. So you can reclaim your peace, recenter yourself, and get back in control.

Stay Calm And Take Your Time

As you can see, what you focus on during a setback can play a significant role in the final results of your project. Plan for setbacks — they will happen — and plan on meeting them head-on while focusing on the end result. You'll find in the end that you're a lot happier and calmer through the entire process.

During a stressful time, meditation actually can calm your head and help you to get more clarity and focus. A simple ten or fifteen-minute breathing exercise or guided meditation can help you to overcome your stress and find some inner peace and balance. There are many great free meditation apps, such as Stop, Breathe & Think and Insight Timer.

Each of the previous scenarios deals with a homeowner who gets a little impatient to get things done doesn't take the time to double check the details and rushes the process. And each one pays the price for their haste. Now you have three examples of what not to do, so heed them and avoid the same pitfalls. Don't be like Joan, Patrick, or Cindy. Be YOU -- the smartest, most strategic version of you. Patience, preparation, and a proactive approach will ultimately pay off. (That's called alliteration!)

Like the great philosopher, Taylor Dayne sang so wisely back in the 80's … "Don't Rush Me."

"Your ability to adapt to failure, and navigate your way out of it, absolutely 100 percent makes you who you are."
- Viola Davis, Actress

Insider Tips

It's easy to be wise after failure. So let's figure out ahead of time ways to avoid project failure. Many professionals practice *premortem* exercises. It's the hypothetical opposite of a postmortem. Imagine all the reasons your project could turn into a miserable failure at the beginning of a project rather than the end. Then figure out how you can prevent those problems so that the project can be improved, while there's still time. Here are the 3 easy steps to conduct this backward perspective towards the future analysis: (1) Plan for unexpected situation or the worst case scenario — focus on showstoppers, pick problems likely to happen, and discard problems you have no control over, (2) Write down all the reasons for failure, (3) Brainstorm with solution

Always plan to have at least a 10% contingency fund. Often there will be a situation where you have no control, e.g., weather condition, etc. Here are the steps to mitigate setbacks by minimizing the unexpected proactively: (a) Keep track the project progress and weather condition, (b) Schedule wisely and minimize scope change, (c) Appropriate procurement timely manner, (d) Proper documentation, (e) Clear and frequent communication, and lastly (f) Paid only when work is completed per contract.

SETBACK PLANNER WORKSHEET

Unexpected Situation/ Worse Case Scenario	Solutions
Example: Downpour during roofing work	Put precious things in storage to prevent water damage. Use tarp to cover remaining areas.

16 Treat Your Team with R-E-S-P-E-C-T, Trust, & Gratitude

It's very easy during home improvements to get laser-focused on the tasks and the end result that you lose sight of other things that are involved, such as the people who are doing the work. Every home improvement project consists of a team of individuals who work hard to bring your goal to fruition.

And while it's understandable that you get so focused on your goal that you sometimes lose sight of smaller issues, it's imperative that you treat every member of your team — including yourself — with respect. Everyone has their own feelings, needs, and fears, so it's important to consider those in each interaction.

Remember, you're all on the same team, and part of being on a team means being aware of your teammates' perspectives. We should be making things better for each other, not making matters worse, and this requires an increased awareness of what each person is dealing with regarding stress, workload, time constraints, and other exterior factors.

Working Together

You hired your Pro to do this job for you, and they have the same goal of successfully completing the project. They're not out to give you a hard time, take advantage of you, or make your life harder than it already is.

So, when your Pro makes a suggestion or tells you that something can't be done the way you initially requested, you need to treat this person with respect. Sure, it might be annoying, but they are just delivering the message, not trying to sabotage your project. You hired them for their expertise, so contradicting them, talking down to them, or dismissing their input is not going to help you reach your end goal.

How would you feel if they treated you that way? (Uh-huh. It wouldn't feel so good, would it?) This person is a member of your team, and they deserve the same respect as you. By taking a collaborative approach and a respectful tone, you can defuse tension and lead by example, making them feel valued, considered, and understood — plus, they'll likely respect you more. They'll also be more likely to listen to your opinions and ideas, and they might even look for ways to make your project even better, instead of just doing the bare minimum. When there's an environment of mutual respect, things go more smoothly for everyone, which is essential to the project's success.

You Need A Little R-E-S-P-E-C-T, Too

Like effective communication, respect goes both ways, so don't be afraid to have a conversation if you're not getting the respect that you're giving. This is your home, and you've done a lot of research and prep for the project, not to mention the fact that you're the one who has to live in the space once it's done, so you need to ensure that you're getting that respect. It's essential to speak up and advocate for your own needs and wishes with your Pro. Your opinions matter and your feedback are crucial, so if you need to have that conversation, do it in the same calm, respectful, and professional manner you'd expect from anyone communicating with you.

Be A 'Learning-It-All,' Instead Of A 'Know-It-All'

You've done a lot of research getting ready for this project, and, hopefully, it has you feeling well-informed and more confident. Just remember, there's a difference between confidence and arrogance. Your Pro will appreciate that you've taken an active hand in learning more, but not if you're acting like you know more than they do.

Nobody wants to work on any project with that person who knows everything about everything. (Remember how annoying Hermione Granger was at the beginning of the *Harry Potter* series? We get it, Hermione — you know *all* the answers.) Similarly, you don't want to be that homeowner who is weighing in on every aspect of the project, offering your input or opinion when it isn't really necessary, just to appear knowledgeable. This may cause your Pro to feel tension, frustration, and resentment … none of which help them do their best work. Instead of being a "know-it-all," strive to be a "learning-it-all" by asking questions and deferring to your Pro's expertise to show them you're taking an active interest in learning more about the process instead of regurgitating facts and stats to show how much you already know. By adopting a learning mindset, not only will you gain some valuable knowledge which you can apply on future projects, but your Pro will respect you even more, which makes for a great working relationship. And your whole project is all about building relationships. It's a real full-circle moment.

When I began my job as a Campus Architect at Berkeley, I was excited — and overwhelmed. I was fresh out of college with very little construction experience, so I went to one of my mentors, Professor Cassandra Adams, for guidance. I remember the exchange in her office like it was yesterday. She said to me, "Be humble, be hungry for knowledge, be fair to others and yourself, and always ask questions when you don't know something." The wisdom of these profound, yet simple lessons have helped me continue to learn and grow in all areas of my life, so I share them with you now with the hopes they will serve you well, too.

Be Humble

Humbling yourself can be one of the most challenging things you'll ever do. It means taking a step back from the situation, acknowledging your faults and lack of knowledge, and admitting that someone else may be better suited to take the lead. To be able to do that isn't admitting weakness; it actually has the strength to defer to someone who is a real subject matter expert and doing it to better serve the project.

Be prepared to humble yourself from time to time — to your designer, your contractor, your installers, your design consultants — and seize it as a learning opportunity. These people are the experts in their fields, that's why you've chosen to work with them. They want to help you realize your vision, and they want your project to be a success, so humble yourself a little and listen to their expertise and experience.

Be Hungry

Being open to others' ideas and opinions doesn't mean that you're taking a passive role in your own project; this is where the idea of balance begins to emerge. You want to stay hungry and maintain engagement in the project as a whole; however, if you put others in front of your wishes too many times, you're going to lose enthusiasm for the project.

Listen to your Pros and experts when they speak. Weigh what they have to say carefully, and integrate it into what you already know. Ask questions, and try to align what you are learning with your ideas. If you find that what they are offering isn't what you want, then it's time to assert yourself. If they have the wrong impression of what you want or what your lifestyle is, respectfully correct them and express your wishes so you can all get on the same page. Be hungry for new knowledge, but know when to share the knowledge you already have with others.

Be Fair

Fairness is the companion of balance. (That's why the phrase is "fair and balanced.") Never dismiss what someone has to say without giving it careful consideration. If you find that your Pro isn't meshing with you, don't just fire them and move on; that's not fair to them, to you, or to your project. Instead, take control and engage in a conversation where you can have an honest exchange of ideas and course correct your relationship. You may find that there was a miscommunication or they had a different understanding of something and that caused the hiccup. Give them the chance to explain and hear them out; it's only fair, and it will help you get back on course.

It's About Balance

Strive for balance in all areas. Find the balance between hands-on and meddling. Inquisitive and nagging. Assertive and overbearing. Don't forget about that balance between humble and hungry so you can go the distance for your project. Remember, it's about being fair to your Pro and fair to yourself.

Leave It To The Pros

TRUST YOUR PROS. You hired them for their expertise, so trust them to put it to work for you to help you realize your vision.

LISTEN TO YOUR PROS. Let them share their expertise with you and learn from them. If they say something won't work, ask questions. Have they encountered this before? Are there similar options that would work? What would they do if it was their own home? Listen and learn from them as you work together to find a solution.

LET YOUR PROS DO THEIR JOB. You've done the research and prep work, hired your team, approved designs and construction plans — now it's time to get the heck out of their way and let them shine. It's time to step back and let them do what they do best. You get to watch their expertise in action. It's okay to communicate and get progress updates, but they don't need babysitting. Of course, if they need you or have any questions, you'll be available to them, but you've handed over the reins to them. Take a deep breath and enjoy the process and the progress!

"I'm a very strong believer in listening and learning from others."
- Ruth Bader Ginsburg, Supreme Court Judge
(A.K.A. Notorious RBG)

Insider Tips

You may love watching the *Game of Thrones* or the other mental chess battles that unfold, but it doesn't mean you want to live through your home improvement project like a full season of the show.

Newton's laws of Action - Reaction, where a collision has resulted in a force being applied to the two colliding things. A reaction is typically quick, without much thought, tense and aggressive. A response is thought out, calm and non-threatening. A reaction

usually provokes more reactions — perpetuating a long line of hatefulness with nothing accomplished. A response typically encourages discussion — perpetuating healthy discussion that leads to resolution. To avoid a potential collision, you can take control and choose to respond, rather than react, with your heart at peace.

PEACE VS. WAR EXERCISE

Building on the story from the previous chapter with Pauline and Jake, do you recall the last time you were upset due to conflict with someone? Why were you upset? Did you see them as a person with feelings, hopes, and fears? Or, did you view them as just an obstacle? How long did it take to resolve the conflict?

The Arbinger Institute book *The Anatomy of Peace* identified two basic principles:

1. When we see others as people — with hopes, needs, and fears that are as real to them as ours are to us, then we treat others as to how we want to be treated with our heart at peace.
2. When we see others as objects — tools to be used, obstacles to our goals, or even irrelevant, then we treat others as enemies, provoking hurtful behavior with our heart at war.

When our hearts are at war, we are unable to see clearly the other person's point of view, and we act in ways that are counterproductive. As a result, we allow our own negative attitudes and behaviors to drive us, forcing us to see others as worse than they really are. Naturally, the other party will react based on their perception of your words and actions. This becomes a vicious cycle, with each side reacting to their words and actions with unkind behavior, causing things to escalate quickly.

We tend to justify our attitudes and behaviors toward others based on three basic needs:

1. To believe that we are better than other people.
2. To believe we deserve more than other people.
3. To be well thought of by other people.

These needs are inward thinking mindset — judging and blaming, and we trapped ourselves in those needs boxes until we recognize their limitations and step outside them to gain a different perspective.

One way to overcome an inward thinking mindset is to pivot to an outward thinking mindset — considering the behavior of others. Here are a few sample questions we can ask ourselves to train our minds to shift outward thinking mindset with a deep understanding and motivation to change:

- What are challenges, fears, burdens, and pains that this person or these people are facing?
- How am I adding to these challenges, fears, burdens, and pains?
- How have I contributed in neglecting or mistreating this person or these people?
- How are my 'better-than,' "I-deserve,' and 'must-be-seen' boxes obscuring the truth about other people and myself and interfering with potential solutions?
- What can I do for this person or these people based on my feeling?
- What can I do to help?

When we are genuinely committed to peacefully collaborating with others - not just to prove ourselves right, we must start with outside-in approach with our attitudes and behaviors that may demonize others and work on to find peace in our hearts. Then, we must build relationships, both with other people who may influence the situation and who we have mistreated as enemies. As we listen to others and learn from those who we have been in conflict, they may be willing to open to our attempts to connect and communicate. When we more fully understand one another, we will be in a much better place to work through things that were going wrong and work together to make things go right.

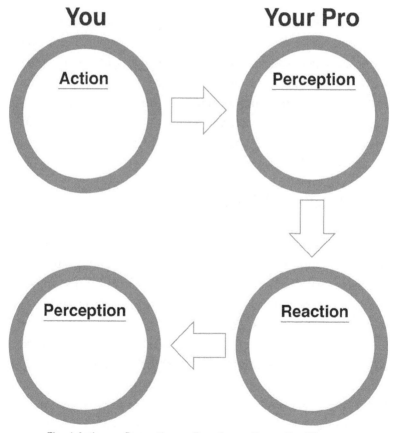

Fig. 4 Action -> Perception -> Reaction -> Perception Diagram.

17 Get on the Same Page

Communication is vital, especially when working with a large team on a home renovation project. Sometimes, the lines of communication get crossed, and the message gets garbled. It happens, we're only human. For example, you may tell your Pro one thing, and your spouse tells an installer something else, resulting in the final action not being what was supposed to happen. This causes frustration, anger, and finger-pointing, in addition to a delay to your project while you rectify the mistake.

Repeat Yourself, If Necessary

You'd like to think that if you've told one person something, then this information will be swiftly and accurately communicated to everyone on the project. Sadly, that's not the world we live in. With so many people and components working on a project, it's easy for miscommunication to occur.

Remember that game called "telephone" that you played in grade school? You whisper something into a friend's ear, then they whisper it to the person next to them, and so one. By the end of the game, the last person hears something very different from what the original message was. That's not how you want people communicating on your project. By telling only one person, you run the risk of your instructions getting miscommunicated over time. Yikes!

For example, if you say that you want 12-inch marble tile in the bathroom, and your Pro tells the installer that you want a large format marble tile in the bathroom, your installer may pick up some 16- or 18-inches tiles for the job. By putting things in writing, you can drive clarity for everyone. Ideally, you have a central hub for this information that everyone can consult to make sure they are getting the correct information. Of course, you can also be that hub and speak directly to each person to give them the info, but that might not be the wisest use of your time.

Communication: Have A Plan

At the earliest opportunity, you and your Pro should agree on the best way to communicate and exchange information, so everyone stays on the same page, and nothing falls through the cracks. Whether it's a group text with all the team members included or a group email, you should have some record of what was said and agreed upon that everyone can refer back to for the sake of clarity. Errors can be spotted more quickly this way, plus, you'll proactively prevent unnecessary conflict and confusion.

Have Weekly Team Updates

Another best practice is to arrange a brief weekly meeting between you and your team. You should include as many team members as possible so you can ...

- Quickly summarize what has already been done & what work remains
- Give status updates for the upcoming week's scheduled work

- Identify any issues or roadblocks that could impede progress or affect timelines
- Create an open forum for any questions or concerns

You can relay any information you might have, and thank everyone for their hard work. (Hot Tip: ordering pizza or bringing doughnuts for the crews ensures higher attendance and will earn you gratitude and hard work. It's a small investment to make, compared to the returns you'll receive.) That way, you can get everyone on the same page, show your appreciation, and boost team morale — everyone wins!

Make Communication The Key

To foster effective communication, you can set the tone by starting with you practicing *The Four Agreements* by Don Miguel Ruiz. These four principles will help you to establish healthy and productive collaborations among the team members, and get everyone on the same page. Here's the *Cliffs Notes* version:

Be Impeccable With Your Word
- Speak with integrity and honesty. Be truthful and say only what you mean.
- We act on what we tell ourselves is real.
- Avoid using the negative Word to speak against yourself or to gossip about others.
- Use the power of positive Word in the direction of truth and love.

Don't Take Anything Personally
- Nothing others do is because of you.
- What others say and do is a projection of their own reality, their own dream.
- When you are immune to the opinions and actions of others, you won't be the victim of needless suffering.

Don't Make Assumptions
- Find the courage to ask questions and to express what you really want.
- Communicate with others as clearly as you can to avoid misunderstandings, sadness and drama.
- With just this one agreement, you can completely transform your life.

Always Do Your Best
- Your best is going to change from moment to moment; it will be different when you are healthy as opposed to sick.
- Under any circumstance, simply do your best, and you will avoid self-judgment, self-abuse, and regret.

Fig. 5 Four Agreements.

Put these principles to work as you navigate your project. Effective communication between you, your team, and your family is essential to a successful outcome.

It's Family Business: Get On The Same Page With Your Family

You would assume that family members want the same things for their home, but that's not always the case. Even if one spouse or partner tells the other that they can have their way, it's very common for two people to give conflicting instructions to a Pro, resulting in frustration and confusion.

We've talked about the importance of communicating with your team, but don't forget that your team includes your family.

Your spouse or partner, as well as your children, are all going to be affected by the renovation process, so make sure you're all on the same page. Make sure that your communication process includes them, so there is no miscommunication with your Pros. Check in frequently, see how they are feeling, and discuss any questions they may have. Anytime you speak to your Pro, it's essential that the other person knows what was considered; this helps avoid any conflict or complications.

The renovation process is stressful, and that stress can affect your relationship and your family ... if you let it. Being without a kitchen or bathroom for days or weeks, living with plastic tarps cutting off your access to certain parts of the home, dealing with the stress of trying to pay for it all, and trying to cope with change orders and strange people in your home every day — all of this is enough to make even the sanest person feel crazy.

It happens far more often than you might think. A couple embarks on a new home improvement project, only to end up fighting and bickering through from start to finish. Even worse, the Pro may get dragged into the middle of it, finding themselves mediating situations that go far beyond the scope of normal home improvement disagreements. This is likely because there's a lack of communication.

Couples may find themselves getting into heated arguments, simply due to the stress of it all. Make sure that both of you are on the same page before you embark on the renovation. If you have differing ideas of how this project is going to turn out, or what your budget is, you're setting yourself up for guaranteed conflict as the project unfolds. Have honest, open, respectful discussions to resolve issues ahead of time and don't proceed until you both agree on what you want out of the project.

Choose Your Battles

Is the color of your new kitchen faucet that important to you? What about the species or origin of your hardwood floor? Are you really willing to go to the mat over a ceramic backsplash behind the stove? Choose your battles! Pick the things that are the most meaningful to you, and cede to the others to your partner. If a gantry style faucet is really going to make a difference in your use of the kitchen, then by all means, stick up for it. But if the issue is merely cosmetic and clearly means more to your partner than to you, then that's not the hill you're willing to die on, so let them have that and keep it moving. Save your energy for something that really matters to you.

Don't Drag Your Pro Into Your Business

Whatever marital or relationship issues this home renovation may bring to light, you need to keep them where they belong: between you and your spouse or partner! **Never drag your Pro into it, never ask them to choose sides.** Your Pro isn't there to referee your disagreements, he's there to do his job according to the agreed-upon design. How would you feel if you got dragged into another couple's squabble or were asked to choose sides between your friends? AWK-WARD! It's a no-win situation, so if you value the outcome of your project, don't put your Pro in this position. Period.

If pressing issues arise during the project, try to come to an agreement on the most time-sensitive ones first. Never bicker or argue in front of your Pro or the rest of the team. If you need to have a discussion, either save it for the end of the day after the crew has left, or excuse yourselves and find somewhere private to hash it out like practicing adults — calmly and respectfully. Keep your lines of communication open, and keep those boundary lines in place with your Pro, and you'll enjoy a much smoother process.

"Coming together is a beginning,
Keeping together is progress,
Working together is success."
- Henry Ford, Founder of the Ford Motor Company

Insider Tips

Communication is an essential process in our everyday life, and your entire project revolves around it. Effective communication builds trust among teammates, encourages increased productivity, and fosters a collaborative environment — all key to achieving project success. It starts working from day one of your project and continues for the entire lifespan of the project. Use the following Get On The Same Page worksheet to help identify who is responsible for providing which type of updates to keep everyone on the project on the same page.

GET ON THE SAME PAGE

Type of Updates	Who	Frequency
Progress		
Changes		
Issues		
Decisions		
Payments		

18   Documentation: How to Stay in Control Without Micromanaging

It's a good rule of thumb to properly document everything, especially when it comes to your renovation project. Doing so creates a record of what was said, what was done, and what was agreed to, which can be incredibly helpful to clarify anything if there is miscommunication. Having proper documentation to refer back to puts you in control, and will save you countless headaches and loads of stress.

You should be documenting any communication between you and the people on your team; emails, text messages, plans, and contracts all serve as written documentation. You should also summarize any conversations you have with your team, especially if they involve any adjustments to the timeline, budget, or original design plan. Ideally, those would all be outlined in writing, but it's a good idea to have contemporaneous documentation or what was said, too.

Document Everything

Documentation is the key to preventing misunderstandings and errors. It's better to discuss it, have everyone on the same page, and have it spelled out in writing so that things get done the first time correctly. I'm not just talking about a sticky note in your Pro's workbook; they should be just as diligent about proper documentation as you are because it protects everyone. This is where that central communication hub I referred to a few chapters ago would come in handy. Whether it's a Google Doc on your Google Drive or other shared drives like iCloud that everyone can access and update, or another tool, this documentation will make your life easier and help your project run smoothly. Let's look at a few scenarios where documentation would have come in handy:

Lisa is at the tile store, selecting a new, handmade tile for her bathroom. She chooses one in a sunny bright yellow shade that fluctuates in color over the surface. She envisions her bathroom looking as though it will be bathed in light.

The tile that arrives at the house is dull yellow on the borderline of orange, but it's not the color she ordered. Since the tile installer was told the tile was yellow, and he saw the dull yellow tiles arrives in the manufacture boxes, so he installs it. When Lisa gets home, she finds that the tile was incorrect, and must now be torn out, reordered, and reinstalled, costing hundreds of dollars, plus hours of work.

If Lisa had taken a picture of the tile and it's SKU or color name and number, photocopied the sample board, or even requested an actual sample to hand to the installer, this could have been avoided. We are all carrying smartphones with HD cameras and mini-supercomputers in our pockets, so that documentation could have been done quickly and easily. Use your smartphone for documenting more than just your avocado toast or your latest selfie.

Martin encountered a different type of documentation problem on his project. In his case, the project was underway when it was discovered that there was an old doorway sealed up in the dining room. Martin wanted it reopened, and he spoke to the Pro. However, the Pro did not document the conversation and started the demolition work.

After the demolition, Martin realized that by doing so it would mean redoing the entire wall, as well as the flooring beneath it, adding thousands of dollars to the job. Because it was not clear to Martin and the Pro didn't document properly, Martin was blindsided by the shocked at the bill that followed. If Martin had insisted on getting a written estimate or a change order for the new project, he would have had more information so he could carefully weigh his decision before deciding to go ahead and spend the extra money.

C.Y.A. — Document, Document, Document!

Is that subtle enough?!? Every time you make a decision about the job, or something about the job changes in some way, it deserves to be documented. Period. That way, you're covered if anything gets called into question. Wouldn't you rather have the specifics of what was said, by whom, on what day if you ever have to refer back to it? As the late, great Whitney Houston said to Diane Sawyer, "Show me the receipts. Show me the receipts!"

There's so much technology available to you to help you simplify the documentation process; you have no excuse not to properly document everything. Keep everything in a file, and share with all involved parties. Never assume that things will go exactly as planned based merely on verbal communication. There are countless moving pieces to your renovation process, and things move quickly. Better to document it and have peace of mind in case you need it. It can save you time, stress, inconvenience, and money. Like a certain athletic apparel company says, just do it.

Be In Control, But Don't Micromanage

It's perfectly reasonable to want to know what's going on with your project and to feel "in the know" on daily progress. What you *don't* want to be is a micromanager. I don't like to be micromanaged, do you? Do you want someone hovering over your every move, continually asking what's going on with everything you do on a daily basis? Nobody likes that. Especially not your Pro.

At its root, micromanagement merelly is about control. The need to feel in control of things going on around you. The need to feel that you know what's going on. The fear that things might fall apart if you don't stay on top of everything. I get it, it's human nature to crave the security that comes from being in control, but micromanagement is not the way to achieve it.

Micromanagement is not going to get you better results or increased productivity. If anything, it will create resentment and tension between you, and it displays a lack of trust and confidence in their ability to do their job. That's insulting to your Pro. Don't be that micromanaging homeowner, be the client they love to collaborate with! Don't hover, don't hound them; you don't have time for that, and they don't have the patience to put up with it. Use your tools and technology to help you feel in control and stay in the loop without looming over their shoulder.

"I think I have a big fear of things spiraling out of control. Out of control and dangerous and reckless and thoughtless scares me, because people get hurt."
- Taylor Swift, Musician

"Life comes with many challenges. The ones that should not scare us are the ones we can take on and take control of."
- Angelina Jolie, Actor, Philanthropist

Insider Tips

From the minute your project starts, e.g., meeting your new Pro, you need to start keeping a good paper trail of all documents, communications, payments, and decisions. It's a good practice to help to move the project forward, and it can also protect you in case there is any conflict.

PAPER TRAIL

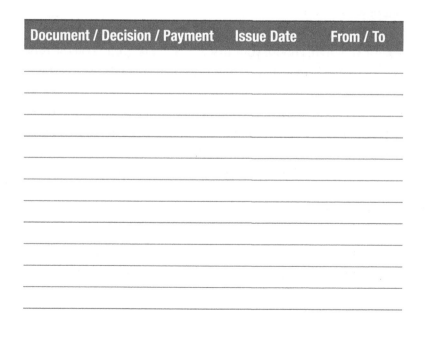

Document / Decision / Payment	Issue Date	From / To

You've Got This

You've done all the prep work, you've identified your WHY/FI and moved past your fear, and you've unlocked your creativity and lined up your squad, prepared yourself to begin your home improvement journey. Now, your project is underway, and maybe you're starting to feel a little unsure; that's perfectly normal because you might not yet understand how you'll react to certain circumstances. Once you start making decisions and the process begins picking up speed, you'll feel your confidence grow, but until then, you may feel little out of your depth.

Nothing can prepare you for how it will feel when you approve your first design, choose your first tile or break ground on the project. You're likely to feel a mixture of excitement and nervous apprehension; after all, this is uncharted territory. The key is to not let those nerves get in the way. While you may have prepared yourself to take those first steps, you may still need a little extra help to psych yourself up and not let your nerves take over during the early stage of your project. What are you going to do? Get your power pose on!

Summoning Confidence

Think about the person you want to be when making your decisions. This person knows what they want in the project. They're capable, they've done their research. They've hired the best Pros and sourced the materials they want for the job. Now it's time to put actual decisions into action, and that person is present, confident, and ready to begin.

How would that person act? What would they say? They would likely be confident and decisive, right? Well, you need to be that person, even if you might not be there just yet. Acting as if you have all the confidence you need — even if you don't feel one hundred percent confident yet — will set the stage for the new and improved you, brimming with confidence and standing in your power.

Strike A Pose!

By all means, envision your completed project; it's good to think ahead and have a positive mindset — just don't dwell on the future at the expense of the present. Staying present in the moment as you work toward your goal is how you're going to achieve it. If you're too focused on what lies ahead, you're likely to overlook the small decisions and choices along the way, which leads to mistakes. Then, those mistakes pile up, and you find your confidence faltering.

Here's a quick and easy hack: adopt a power pose! Your physical posture governs how you think and feel about yourself, and therefore, how you hold your body can have an impact on your state of mind. In Amy Cuddy's book *Presence*, she shared the evidence of high-power posing, where you extend your arms with expansive posture like Diana, Princess of the Amazons (a.k.a. Wonder Woman), for two minutes, you can get yourself to feel more powerful and summon the confidence within.

Guess what? You're probably already power posing, only you don't even realize it. Every time you take a selfie, you're power posing. You're visualizing the most photogenic version of yourself, summoning the extra confidence to see and project yourself at your most glamorous, finding your best light and angle, and taking multiple shots to get the perfect picture. Spoiler alert: you're power posing.

As you move through the project, getting more confident with each decision you make, you'll find that your power pose becomes less of a pose in the pretending sense, because you've got that confidence now. You're in control and working with your Pros to make your project a success.

This Is Your Moment

It's go time! All your hard work and preparation is about to pay off, as your project begins and your home transformation goes from paper to palpable. This is the time to be excited and get into an enthusiastic, positive headspace. Be proud of all the work you've put in, and be excited for all the work that you're about to do. Meet any misgivings or apprehension about the project head-on, then work through them. You've got the tools, and you know what to do. This isn't the time for doubt, it's time to G.S.D. (Get Sh*t Done)! You've worked hard for this. This is your moment; savor it. I'll be right over here, chilling the champagne to toast you.

"It is not the critic who counts; not the man who points out how the strong man stumbles, or where the doer of deeds could have done them better. The credit belongs to the man who is actually in the arena, whose face is marred by dust and sweat and blood; who strives valiantly; who errs, who comes short again and again, because there is no effort without error and shortcoming; but who does

actually strive to do the deeds; who knows great enthusiasms, the great devotions; who spends himself in a worthy cause; who at the best knows in the end the triumph of high achievement, and who at the worst, if he fails, at least fails while daring greatly, so that his place shall never be with those cold and timid souls who neither know victory nor defeat."
\- Theodore Roosevelt, 26th U.S. President

"Action is the foundational key to all success."
\- Pablo Picasso, Artist

Insider Tips

You've become powerful, and you've got this. So unleash your inner genius. Take a moment to jot down the critical components of your project. Soon you'll see how much you've learned, and how confident you are as you embark on your renovation journey.

UNLEASH YOUR INNER GENIUS

Your WHY/FI
Your Squad
Your Budget
Your Schedule
Your Terms

PART IV

Oh, One
More Thing

20 Prep Yourself with the Right Tools

Life in the digital age is pretty good. You've got thousands of sources for inspiration, information, and ideas for your home improvement project, both online and onscreen. Gone are the days when you only had a handful of choices for your home, as well as the days when you'd have to spend hours physically writing down all the details you could remember as you attempt to create a system for managing your renovation process.

Now, more than any other time in recorded history, you have more information, technology, and tools at your fingertips — literally. There are much easier ways to take control of your renovation, track every detail, every communication, every change, and even pay for completed work. With myriad apps available, you can find several to keep track of everything from your smartphone.

APPSolutley Essential: Make Use of Every Tool

Today, you can find apps that will tell you the best position of a new window in your home to get the best light. There are apps with messaging systems that will keep your entire team linked together easily. You've got apps that allow you to virtually design and decorate a home room by room, selecting wall colors and placing fixtures.

That's why I find it interesting that homeowners who spend hours researching and drawing inspiration from photos and images online before beginning their project, often fail to put the available high-tech tools to work once their project is underway. Why stop now? Why not make your life easier and take a little unnecessary stress away? There's no reason to stand on the sidelines, waiting for Pros to drive the project. I want you to step up and take an active hand in managing your renovation, using as many of the available tools you can find.

Prepare Yourself To Enjoy the Journey

Even though your Pro is taking point and running the process, your participation is far from over; you have countless choices and decisions to make in the coming weeks, from materials, to paint colors, to the final placement of fixtures. Using whatever tools are available to you is one way that you can help make these decisions with authority.

From the first glimpse of a new home improvement project on the distant horizon, all the way to its successful completion, it's a long, arduous journey. Along the way, you'll experience growth, self-discovery, frustration, and fun. Just take things step by step and enjoy the journey, 'cuz Rome wasn't built in a day, and — despite what many HGTV shows would have you believe — neither will your project.

Renovations often take weeks, even months to complete. While not every moment of this time is going to involve construction, you need to keep in mind that things will start to move quickly and there will be more and more details to keep track of as the process picks up steam.

This is when you will need to get your tools lined up and get ready to use them. Why use outdated analog methods when you have high tech tools to maximize your time? The whole idea is to work smarter, not harder. There is a wide range of options available, allowing you to pick which apps work best for you and your style. Do some exploring, read the reviews, try some out and see if you like them.

Let BEYREP Help

Based on my own home improvement nightmare, I created BEYREP — a personalized online home improvement tool for busy people like you. Based on the problems I encountered, I wanted to create a comprehensive tool to specifically address and solve those problems so other homeowners will have all the tools I wished I'd had. It's designed to simplify the entire process, from finding a Pro to tracking every detail. It matches you with qualified, vetted, and compatible professionals based on your project type, your preference, and your personality. Think of it as a matchmaker and wedding planner for home improvement projects.

It's a complete home improvement management resource that removes the struggle and frustration of trying to keep track of everything, and it puts the process in your hands. It's a central hub that allows you to manage the process from start to finish, from finding a Pro to checking off milestones, to making secure payments to your team. It packs all that power and puts it in the palm of your hand.

Get A Personalized Match With Compatible Pros

One of the most critical components for any home improvement project is selecting the right Pro. It seems like you need to call at least six of them just to get three to come by for an estimate. Then, you need to follow up on references, credentials, licenses, and businesses before you can even start considering whether you think one of them is right for the job. In short, it's a lot of work and a lot of time.

BEYREP cuts through all of this by matching you up with a Pro who works on your type of home, your type of style, is aligned with your preference, and who matches your personality type, so you know this will be a compatible match. Best of all, you can connect with your matched pros, and get straight to the heart of your project without spending time calling one by one from a directory list.

You just answer some simple questions about the nature of your project, where you're located, and what you want to have done. That's it. Once you're matched, you can communicate with them through the system to streamline the process and keep a record of your interactions. When you're ready, select your Pro to work through the scope and timing of your project.

Then your Pro will provide a detailed project schedule and cost break out for your project so you can track the progress when you are ready to hire. BEYREP has handled the vetting of our Pros so you can connect with confidence. That's an easy way to save a whole block of time and frustration. Boom!

Manage the Project Anytime, Anywhere

No matter how big or small, any home improvement project comes with a paper trail — and a lot of administrative headaches. You need to keep track of who's doing what work and when, whether or not supplies have been ordered or delivered, whether changes have been made to the original contract, and whether the work is getting done on the proposed schedule or not. (Remember Chapter 18? BEYREP is the central hub that helps you "DOCUMENT, DOCUMENT, DOCUMENT!")

It's not realistic to put the rest of your life on hold while this is going on, which is why BEYREP makes it simple to stay hands-on and handle the situation. Upload all of your information to the cloud, then access it anywhere — home, the office, the beach — all on your schedule, on demand, and at your fingertips so you and your Pro can always ensure you're on the same page.

Secure, Escrow-esque Payments

It's every homeowner's worst nightmare — a Pro takes your money but never finishes the job. Protect yourself and your assets with BEYREP's secure online payment, so you never have to worry about this again. Once you've agreed to hire the Pro, based on the proposed detailed estimate, it will convert to an agreement. Upload the agreed upon project budget and scope of work, you'll deposit funds per phase to the account, so your Pro can start of the project. The funds are held while your Pro is working, so you'll never have to worry that your Pro will take the money and run, without completing the agreed work.

Although we're not an escrow service, that's basically how this functions, adding another layer of security to safeguard your money. Now, you can make sure the job is done properly before you release the money so you can protect yourself and your assets while ensuring that your project gets done the right way.

Once the Pro completes each phase, you'll receive a payment release request from your Pro. You'll even have a chance to review the quality of the work before your approval of releasing the payment for that phase; this protects both you and the Pro, as you only release the funds once the phase has been completed to your satisfaction. Work gets done, the Pro gets paid, everybody wins!

Change Is Inevitable

If changes need to be made to the original plan, these change orders will be created in the system for your approval by the Pro. Once you approve them, they'll be able to get started. No more miscommunication or wondering what the status is. You've got the info you need in the palm of your hand. (Or the desktop version of the tool, too.)

Once the project is complete, you'll be encouraged to complete a Punch List with the Pro to make the final walk through and take care of all those little final details. As soon as you're satisfied, you'll release the final funds, and close out the project. You will always have access to your project information — anytime, anywhere.

You and your Pro will have access to the same information, and the central communication hub makes sure no messages get missed. Plus, all messages are time-stamped so you can refer specifically to the timeline to avoid any "he said, she said" drama. This transparency creates both increased accountability, and increased collaboration, trust, and communication.

While developing BEYREP, I learned so many more things, and it compelled me to share that knowledge with you, which is why I wrote this book. This book is designed to help you prepare — mentally, emotionally, and strategically. It's intended to be a field guide of sorts. Heck, call it a roadmap! It's here to show you what lies ahead and to help you chart your course so that you won't be shocked by anything you'll encounter along this journey.

Now that you've finished the book, you're ready to hit the ground running — and BEYREP is the perfect solution to help. Your home improvement will be easier and more successful — period. You and your Pro will maximize your TIME and save you MONEY, streamlining your communication and using technology to REVIVIFY your collaboration.

Home improvements can be stressful, but with BEYREP, you'll be in control and have the peace of mind and confidence to enjoy your project. You'll find more detailed information on <u>BEYREP.com</u>. Home improvements with confidence and peace of mind — that's the BEYREP way.

Your mindset determines your outlook,
Your outlook determines your output,
Your output determines your future outcome.

Are you ready to get started? Everything you need is waiting for you in BEYREP. Let's go!

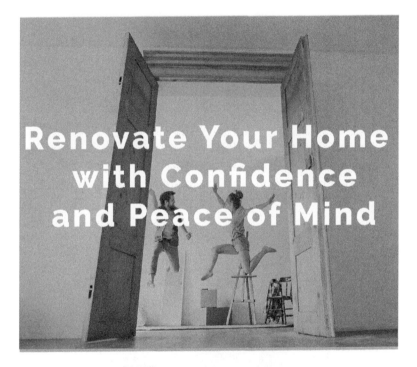

Dream Homes Do Come True with BEYREP

BEYREP understand that home improvements represent a significant emotional and financial investment. We help you avoid the heartache when building or renovating your home. We're professionally trained and our expertise will help you avoid costly mistakes. BEYREP's easy to use system puts you in control to complete your project confidently and successfully. We give you peace of mind as you create your future home.

MANAGE YOUR HOME IMPROVEMENT PROJECT - ANYWHERE AND ANYTIME WITH EASE.

BEYREP is like a "Matchmaker + Wedding Planner + Security guard"
The leading online platform for home improvements

Matchmaking

Get matched with compatible trustworthy professionals

BEYREP's smart matchmaking system connects home owners with suitable home improvement professionals to achieve project success.

Project Management

Track and manage all project related tasks

BEYREP's online platform provides complete transparency throughout the life-cycle of your project to minimize unwanted mistakes.

Secure Payments

Avoid the common risks of overpaying and under-deliver

BEYREP's payment processing system safeguards your investment until completion of your home improvement project.

Get Started and Sign Up For Free Today!

WeCare@BEYREP.COM   877.588.0756   © 2019 BEYREP INC. ALL RIGHTS RESERVED. PATENTED TECHNOLOGY.

"First, have a definite, clear practical ideal; a goal, an objective. Second, have the necessary means to achieve your ends; wisdom, money, materials, and methods. Third, adjust all your means to that end."
- Aristotle, Philosopher

"The journey of a thousand miles begins with one step."
- Lao Tzu, Philosopher

I want to sincerely THANK YOU for your time and your trust. I hope you've gained some knowledge from this that will help your renovation go off without a hitch. I'd love to see and hear about your success, so please hit me up on Facebook or Instagram. Along with the entire team at BEYREP, we're here to support you through every step of your journey.

Appendix: Home Construction Checklist

Home improvements and home renovations often involve more than you may think when you're first starting out. From planning the project to overseeing the work, there's a lot of general detail you'll need to keep track of. While not every piece your project will need to be overseen by you, nor do you need to stay on top of every little detail, it's important to have a general idea of what's going to happen.

This checklist is designed to give you a good starting point for your renovation. Feel free to modify it as needed to suit your particular needs and building goals, and to show it to your Pro as you go to make sure you're both on the same page. The goal of using a checklist is to help you navigate the project smoothly and easily; take a look to get started.

Planning Stages

- Determine whether the project is cosmetic, a full renovation, partial renovation, home repair, or new construction
- Visit your town hall to find out what the regulations are for your project, if permits are required, and what is necessary to obtain them
- Gather ideas for what you are planning including:
  - Magazine photos
  - Color samples

- Material samples
- Pinterest boards
- Houzz Ideaboard
- Instagram
- HGTV shows

⤶ Make a list of all areas of the home you plan on renovating including:
- Kitchen
- Bathroom
- Mudroom
- Bedroom
- Attic
- Basement
- Bedrooms
- Dining Room
- Living Room

⤶ Start the search for your Pro. Use our system to make the search easier, or begin screening, including obtaining:
- Copies of licenses
- Portfolios
- References
- Quotes or bids for the job

⤶ Have the plans and contracts drawn up for review. Be sure to include things like:
- Total project cost
- Material allowances
- Time frame from ground breaking
- The party responsible for pulling permits
- The party responsible for purchasing and acquiring all building materials, including fixtures and finishing items
- Payment schedule and terms
- Hiring of subcontractors, plumbers, electricians and carpenters
- Waste disposal

- ⭦ Approve/sign off on the contracts or plans, or make necessary changes with your Pro
- ⭦ Arrange for financing
- ⭦ Select materials including:
    - Floor finishes (e.g. wood, tiles, etc.)
    - Countertop materials
    - Cabinet materials
    - Crown molding and trim
    - Baseboard moldings
    - Type and size of windows
    - Wall finishes
    - Ceiling finishes
    - Paint colors
    - Cabinet hardware
    - Door & windows
    - Window treatments
    - Light fixtures
    - Appliances
    - Shutters
    - Roofing materials
    - Decking materials
    - Bathroom fixtures and faucets
    - Kitchen fixtures and faucets
    - Fireplace surround tile or mantel and hearth
    - Metal + Stainless Works
    - Wood Works
    - Interior Finishing
- ⭦ Ensure all fixtures, plumbing and electrical appliances are code compliant with your area, get documentation from the manufacturer if necessary

Managing the Project

- Oversee purchasing of all materials and get estimated lead and arrival times, or arrange for this with your Pro
- Schedule work on the house to begin as soon as all materials have arrived at the house, and they have been inspected
- Open all boxes of material as they arrive to double check color, material, and quantity to ensure they are correct. Send back or make arrangements to fix any mistakes
- Clearly label all boxes and move them to the relevant rooms, such as "backsplash material" to the kitchen
- Arrange for alternate sleeping, eating, bathing, and cooking arrangements as necessary while renovations are taking place. Be sure to include contingency plans in case these arrangements go on for longer than planned for
- Arrange for dumpsters, trash removal or removal of debris, or check with your Pro about their arrangement
- Walk through the project with your Pro before it begins, double checking any plans, materials, and placement, and be prepared for change orders as they come up
- Check in frequently with your Pro to ensure the project is moving on schedule and make sure he or she has everything necessary.
- Inspect each finished stage of the project as it's finished, sign off with the Pro if acceptable, and release payments at scheduled milestones
- Take photographs of any issues that arise to have documentation in case of later conflicts

Finishing the Project

- Take a final walkthrough with your Pro
- nspect all finish work, check for issues, missing finish work, chipped materials, and other things that need to be addressed before signing off

- Check all light switches and faucets by turning them on and off. Flush all of the toilets and go to the lowest level of the home to check for leaks after about 10 minutes
- Check to make sure all debris and construction materials have been cleared from the property
- Schedule your inspection with the town
- Sign off on the project with your Pro, and release the final payments

Let BEYREP Help

Managing your home improvements can be a full-time job. That's why BEYREP project management system can help. We'll make the process easy for you and your Pros to communicate and track changes and progress, so you can get time back to focus on your life, comfortable that your project is proceeding on track.

"Finish each day and be done with it. You have done what you could. Some blunders and absurdities no doubt crept in; forget them as soon as you can. Tomorrow is a new day. You shall begin it serenely and with too high a spirit to be encumbered with your old nonsense."
- Ralph Waldo Emerson, Philosopher and Poet

Acknowledgements

Managing your home improvements can be a full-time job. That's why BEYREP project management system can help. We'll make the process easy for you and your Pros to communicate and track changes and progress, so you can get time back to focus on your life, comfortable that your project is proceeding on track.

I'm incredibly fortunate to be surrounded by amazing people who inspire, motivate, encourage, and help me to show up as my best-self every day. There are no words or gifts sufficient to express my gratitude to all of them, but I would start by thanking ...

My incredible & supportive husband, Bob, who inspires me every day, encourages me to get back up when I fall and lifts me up to my highest potential. He has made this journey extraordinary. I can't thank him enough for everything he has done for me.

My best creations, Aidan and Amber, who challenge and motivate me to be a better person. They helped me to find meaning in our contribution to our community, and for us to build a better future for many generations to come. I'm truly grateful and forever in your debt.

Thank you to my parents, who provided the environment for me to push my boundary of curiosity. I learned so much about myself from many of my childhood explorations ... from visiting construction job sites from Taipei to Tunisia ... to tinkering with anything that can be taken apart, from dolls to radios.

Long before there was even an idea of a book, there were amazing professors and classmates who are extraordinary talented architects: Cassandra Adams, Phil Bernstein, June Grant, Mignon O'Young, Catherine Truman, Ghiora Aharoni, Frederick Cook, Chris McIntire, and Mason Kirby, who all shared their brilliant insights during the early stages when I started building BEYREP. I learned so much from them. The fact that BEYREP was built on a solid foundation of fostering positive partnerships and deepening the collaboration between homeowners, design, and building professionals to deliver their shared vision is no accident.

Thank you to each one of the talented and dedicated teammates at BEYREP for pulling me forward. I really appreciate our tech leads Vasyl Berezovyy and Mykola Basov helping me to find ways to improve our user experience. The insights from the projects completed through BEYREP enabled me to appreciate the level of complexity and various friction points along many home improvement journeys, all of which inspired me to begin writing this book. I'm grateful to Beth Asaff, who contributed to the BEYREP blog posts and this book. Her experience as a kitchen and bathroom designer provided great perspective and valuable insights into the common issues in the industry. The reality is that home improvement is not a sexy topic for most people who are not in the industry, but with the support of my teammates, they helped to make it exciting and interesting.

With the help of my incredible editor, Bryan Carpender, we made this book far more interesting and fun than a textbook. I can't thank him enough. As an immigrant, English is my second language. Writing a book was not my core competency, but it's one of my stretch aspiration goals. He was able to help me find my voice — and fought to maintain it throughout the process. He's a decisive editor and a wordsmith, and together, we shaped this into a fun and engaging read. He made this entire editing process collaborative and invigorating.

My incredible coach, Carly Evestien, who saw my potential, challenged me and pushed me to the edge of my potential. She helped me to quiet my self-doubt, confront my limited beliefs, and showed me the path to my best self.

I'm grateful for my awesome patent attorneys Cort Wetherald and Rich Christiansen, who helped me to protect the business process for BEYREP to gain the learning to develop this book. Rich Yu for holding the creative space for me to explore design ideas and being the sounding board with this book cover design.

My #SQUAD, the countless friends who believed in me, and gave me an early break that I needed to get started with this journey, and continue to support me. They took a chance on me, letting me test out my early hypotheses on their home improvement projects. Without them, neither BEYREP nor this book would be where they are today. Rae Lynne Cook, Joaquin Cornejo, Christy Davis, Truc and Frank Moore, Maria and Niels Larsen, Byron and Veronica Darrah, Charita Thakkar, Gokul Hemmady, Lauren Blankenship, Wendy O'Brien, Francisco Cabrera, Angelique and John Quan, Anna and JR Veingkeo, Daniel and Sha Ranchez, Sarah and Dinesh Sadhwani, Ravi Brar, Amandeep and Raj Dhillon, Rich and Jenny Yu, Jerry Cheng, Loc Tran, Tony Petrossian, Mark Ryan, Mina Kuper, Kristy LoRusso, Todd Chittick, Zion Hen, Kika Keith, Rich Yu, Courtney Poulos, Zafar and Vanessa Alikhan, Brenda and Dan Radmacher, and Sally Jue.

Great friends like Julie Campistron, Patrick Southall, Dave Smith, Art Besina, Kurt Mortensen, Colin Giffen, Lorena Arce, Luz Plaza, Gene Chuang, Peter Thornburgh, Dorian DeVries, Mary Lou Branch, Bryan Carney, Charles L. Black III, Stefanie Fujinami, Ian Henzel, Mina Kuper, Veronika Kral, Deborah Deras, Oliver Shay, Rosa Sheng, Yoko Shimm, Joe Radabaugh, all of whom introduced me to their respective networks during my research. My deepest gratitude to my #SQUAD for helping me to learn and for providing valuable feedback for me to refine my hypothesis and improve my theories. They've bent over backward for me. I couldn't ask for better friends and clients!

I'm very grateful to all of the design and building professionals who joined BEYREP in the early stages and helped many homeowners to achieve their home improvement dreams. With their relentless support and guidance, they enabled me to pursue and advance my calling. Thank you to Wyatt Stewart, Vanz Steimle, and Mike Smith of California Pools; Eric Lin of LineWork Development; Susan Sawasy of Casawasy Design; Richard Herb and Connor Jones of Richard Herb and Associates; Tom Christopoulos of Diamond Construction; Steve Mizuki of Mizuki Architect, Maurice Levitch of Levitech Design Build; Oren Farkash of Southland Remodeling; Michelle Andersen of Flourish By Design; Luciana Tagliaferri of Tagliaferri Architects; Ghiora Aharoni of Ghiora Aharoni Design Studio; Chris Mandalian of Mann Build; John Stewart of Stewart & Associates; Whitney Sander of Sander Architects; John Ferri of Spec Concept; Sandra Costa of Sandra Costa Design; Matteo Bitetti; Hamlet Khachikian; Guillame Lemoine of Picture This Land; Lupe Perez of Green Splendor Landscaping; Uzi, Zaray of Ground Up Builders; Ben and Elinor Benhamo of Total Construction and Remodeling; Amy and Sara Phillips of Ridgeline Renovations. They went above and beyond. I'm touched beyond words, extremely humbled, and grateful for their help.

There are a few books that have offered new perspectives and have influenced my thinking and how I see and understand the world around us. I'm grateful for teaching: Creativity, Inc. by Ed Catmull and Amy Wallace; Daring Greatly; Rising Strong, and The Power of Vulnerability by Brené Brown; Start with Why by Simon Sinek; Find Your Why by Simon Sinek, David Mead, and Peter Docker; Purposeful by Jennifer Dulski; Presence by Amy Cuddy; You Are a Badass by Jen Sincero; Emotional Intelligence by Daniel Goleman; The Oz Principle by Roger Connors, Tom Smith, and Craig Hickman; The Four Agreements by Don Miguel Ruiz; Good to Great by Jim Collins; The Universe in a Single Atom by Dalai Lama; Enchantment by Guy Kawasaki; Positive Intelligence by Shirzad Chamine; Originals by Adam Grant and Sheryl Sandberg; The ONE Thing by Gary Keller and Jay Papasan; Blink and David and Goliath by Malcolm Gladwell; The FIve Dysfunctions of a Team by Patrick Lencioni; The Power of Habit by Charles Duhigg; Mindset by Carol Dweck; Grit by Angela Duckworth; The Universe Has Your Back by Gabrielle Bernstein; Find Your Extraordinary by Jessica Dilullo Herrin; and The Anatomy of Peace by Arbinger Institute. As Sir Francis Bacon stated, "Knowledge is power."

"A picture is worth a thousand words." Icons are fantastic depictions of complicated concept in a simple and straightforward interpretation through lines. The objective of this book is to walk you through a complicated process through an uncomplicated flow. Special thanks for both Freepik and Flaticon for sharing these great icons.

Finally, I want to thank you for letting me be part of your journey and improving the environment around you. I hope you'll pay it forward and share the knowledge in this book with others who may be inspired by you, and want to improve their home.

Yours truly,

Grace Tsao Mase

Notes

INTRODUCTION

4   *Did you know home improvement construction has ranked as one of the top three consumer complaints for over twenty years, and for the past six years, has been ranked #2 on the list:* Consumer Federation of America, 2017 Consumer Complaint Survey Report, July 30, 2018, https://consumerfed.org/wp-content/uploads/2018/07/2017-consumer-complaint-survey-report.pdf.

4   *Considering homeowners spend more than $300 billion a year on residential renovations:* Abbe Will, Harvard Joint Center for Housing Studies, *Home Remodeling Expected to Remain Strong and Steady Into 2019,* April 19, 2018, http://www.jchs.harvard.edu/blog/home-remodeling-expected-to-remain-strong-and-steady-into-2019/.

CONNECT YOUR WHY/FI

8   *A very wise man named Simon Sinek is going to help kick off your journey: "Start with WHY.":* Simon Sinek, *Start with WHY,* Portfolio, September 23, 2009.

8   *He explained why it's essential to start with WHY, and it inspired me to participate in the "Finding Your WHY" workshop with Jen Waldman, Peter Docker and Christina Alessi to articulate my WHY:* Simon Sinek, David Mead, and Peter Docker, *Finding Your WHY,* Portfolio, September 5, 2017.

WHOSE ELEPHANT IS THIS?!?

20   *Once you identify the fears that prevent you from moving forward, you can begin to address them:* Shirzad Chamine, Positive Intelligence, Greenleaf Book Group Press, April 3rd 2012.

24 *To get to the root of the issue and take control back from your subconscious mind, you need to decisively name what you're afraid of so you can put together a plan to move past it*: Shirzad Chamine, *Positive Intelligence*, Greenleaf Book Group Press, April 3rd 2012.

25 *"It is impossible to live without failing at something, unless you live so cautiously that you might as well not have lived at all, in which case you have failed by default."* - J. K. Rowling, Author, *Very Good Lives:* Copyright © J.K. Rowling 2008.

KNOW THYSELF!

28 *Consider this fact: while marriages last on average only about 8 years*: Rose M. Kreider and Renee Ellis, United States Census Bureau, *Number, Timing, and Duration of Marriages and Divorces: 2009, Current Population Reports*, May 2011, https://www.census.gov/prod/2011pubs/p70-125.pdf.

28 *Average U.S. homeowner keeps their home for about 15 years*; 2017 National Association of REALTORS, *Home Buyer and Seller Generational Trends Report 2018*, March 14, 2018, https://www.nar.realtor/sites/default/files/documents/2018-home-buyers-and-sellers-generational-trends-03-14-2018.pdf

28 DISC model is a behavior personality assessment tool based on the work of psychologist William Marston's "The Emotions of Normal People" in 1928, which centers on four different personality traits which are: Dominance (D), Inspiring (I), Supportive (S), and Cautious (C). The foundation of the DISC Model is based on two observations about how people usually behave. William Marston, *The Emotions of Normal People*, 1928.

32 *The MBTI was constructed by Katharine Cook Briggs and her daughter Isabel Briggs Myers. It is based on the conceptual theory proposed by Carl Jung, based on the four principal psychological functions – sensation, intuition, feeling, and thinking*: The Myers & Briggs Foundation, *MBTI® Basics, The purpose of the Myers-Briggs Type Indicator*, https://www.myersbriggs.org/my-mbti-personality-type/mbti-basics/home.htm.

36 *The Big Five personality traits were identified by Ernest Tupes and Christal in the late 1950s. They defined five factors, represented by the acronym OCEAN: Openness to experience, Conscientiousness, Extraversion, Agreeableness, and Neuroticism*: Benjamin P. Chapman and Lewis R. Goldberg, University of Rochester School of Medicine and Oregon Research Institute, *Big*

Five: Act-frequency signatures of the Big Five, November 4, 2016, https://projects.ori.org/lrg/PDFs_papers/Chapman&Goldberg_2017_ActFrequencySignaturesBig5_PAID.pdf.

CHECK THE REARVIEW MIRROR BEFORE YOU MOVE FORWARD

50 *Studies have shown that natural light can have many positive benefits, affecting mental health, positively altering your mood, and helping to expedite recovery from illness:* Carla Davis, *Shining Light on What Natural Light Does For Your Body*, North Carolina State University, Sustainability Office, March 24, 2014, https://sustainability.ncsu.edu/blog/changeyourstate/benefits-of-natural-light.

SUSTAINABILITY IS SEXY

72 *From the rising costs of energy to a need to be more conscious about the choices being made for materials in the home, many homeowners starting a home renovation project are taking the time to consider sustainable (energy efficient) design and use the eco-friendly material:* Margaret Robertson, *Sustainability Principles and Practice*, Routledge, March 15, 2017.

74 *Studies have shown that for every dollar you spend on home improvements to increase the energy efficiency of your home, you'll save seven dollars on your energy bills:* Taren O'Connor and William E. Dornbos, *Connecticut Energy Efficiency Board, 2017 Programs and Operations Report*, MARCH 1, 2018, https://www.energizect.com/sites/default/files/Final-2017-Annual-Legislative-Report-WEB-2-20-18.pdf.

74 *Creating An Efficient Home:* James R. Mihelcic and Julie B. Zimmerman, *Environmental Engineering: Fundamentals, Sustainability, Design*, Wiley; January 13, 2014.

MAKE IT HAPPEN

87 *The only difference was in how you approached it:* Shirzad Chamine, *Positive Intelligence*, Greenleaf Book Group Press, April 3rd 2012.

87 *Change the Way You Think:* Carol Dweck, *Mindset: The New Psychology of Success*, Ballantine Books, December 26, 2007.

89 *The spring and the fall are the two busiest times of year for home improvement projects This is because many homeowners are influenced by things like culture, advertising, and subtle forms of peer pressure to get things done on a set schedule:* Becky Goldfarb, Managing Director, Retail

Valuations, Home Improvement Retailers Industry Insight, August 2018, http://www.gordonbrothers.com/insights/industry-insights/retail-home-improvement

93 *Set at least a loose budget for your project; you can fine tune it after you speak to your Pro and they give you more specifics:* Daniel Bortz, *How to set your budget for a big home improvement project*, March 27, 2018, https://www.washingtonpost.com/lifestyle/home/how-to-set-your-budget-for-a-big-home-improvement-project/2018/03/26/acf2b7cc-2c7f-11e8-b0b0-f706877db618_story.html?utm_term=.49e7d84ef337

95 *A contingency fund allows you to have a little bit of peace of mind as you enter a large home improvement project. This is a portion of your budget that is earmarked just for potential problems or issues that may pop up once the project is underway:* David Hodges, *How to budget for home improvement like a pro*, MoneySense, Jan 12, 2017, https://www.moneysense.ca/spend/real-estate/renovations/budgeting-home-improvement.

GET INSPIRED, BE A CREATIVE BADASS, GET YOUR SQUAD, AND ROLL

102 *Search tips:* Google Search Helps, https://support.google.com/websearch/answer/1325808

113 *Hiring the right Pros for your project requires proper research and vetting. You want to assemble the best squad you can, and that means putting in some time and effort on the front end to avoid disaster later:* Kiplinger's Personal Finance, *How to Vet a Contractor*, November 2017, https://www.kiplinger.com/article/real-estate/T029-C000-S002-how-to-vet-a-contractor.html

115 *Getting Background Information;* DMV, https://www.dmv.org/criminal-records.php.

119 "Imagination is more important than knowledge. Knowledge is limited. Imagination encircles the world". Interview of Einstein by G. S. Viereck, Macauley, October 29, 1929 and published in Glimpses of the Great, 1930.

I'LL TELL YOU WHAT I WANT, WHAT I REALLY REALLY WANT

124 *A successful negotiation isn't one where only you get your way; it's when both sides feeling as though they got what they were after, or at least close to it:* Roger Fisher, William L. Ury, and Bruce Patton, *Getting to Yes*, Penguin Books; Updated, Revised edition, 1981.

124 *To prevent negotiations from breaking down before it even begins, it's import-*
     ant that you go in with an understanding of the issues from all perspectives:
     William Ury, *Getting Past No*, Bantam, September 1991.

125 *In the negotiation, you should always be ready and willing to concede something*
     meaningful, but that doesn't jeopardize your end goal: Daniel Goleman,
     Emotional Intelligence, Bantam Books, November 15, 1995.

128 *Successful negotiators know when — and how — to say no*: William Ury, *The*
     Power of a Positive No, Bantam; December 26, 2007.

BE CLEAR AND GET REAL: COMMUNICATE YOUR WHY/FI

138 *I remembered a powerful old story told by an Architectural History Professor*
     Vincent Scully about three bricklayers for the St. Paul's Cathedral in London.
     When the architect Sir Christopher Wren was inspecting the progress of the
     construction, he asked three bricklayers, "What are you doing?" The first man
     said that he was laying bricks. Then the second man answered that he was
     putting up a wall. Lastly, the third man responded that he was building a place
     of worship. Vincent Scully, Yale Art History Professor, Course: History
     of Art 112a, 1998

139 *John F. Kennedy visited NASA and saw a janitor mopping up the floor. JFK*
     asked him what his job was at NASA and the gentleman replied, "I'm helping
     send a man to the moon.": John Nemo, *What a NASA janitor can teach us*
     about living a bigger life, The Business Journal, Dec 23, 2014, https://
     www.bizjournals.com/bizjournals/how-to/growth-strategies/2014/12/
     what-a-nasa-janitor-can-teach-us.html

141 *California had set a limit to 10% or $1,000 or whichever is less for an ini-*
     tial deposit: California Contractors State License Board (CSLB), August
     15, 2012, http://www.cslb.ca.gov/Media_Room/Press_Releases/2012/
     August_15.aspx.

142 *Protect yourself now by learning to know the two kinds of liens*: Investopedia,
     Construction Lien, https://www.investopedia.com/terms/c/construction-
     lien.asp.
     FindLaw, *Understanding Mechanic's Liens*, https://realestate.findlaw.com/
     owning-a-home/understanding-mechanic-s-liens.html.

WHAT TO EXPECT WHEN YOU'RE NOT EXPECTING

153 *A perfect example of the importance of mental preparation is Qantas Airlines*
     Flight 32 in 201. The aircraft used for this flight was an Airbus A380, this